PRAISE FOR THE IN BETWEEN

This is a beautiful deconstruction of a massive adventure, from her heart to paper via all the emotions available.

— SARAH MARQUIS, NATIONAL GEOGRAPHIC EXPLORER, ADVENTURER, AND AUTHOR OF *WILD BY NATURE*

Jenn's journey from fear to courage is highly inspiring. A unique book that helps us be more adventurous.

— FRANCESC MIRALLES, CO-AUTHOR OF THE INTERNATIONAL BESTSELLER *IKIGAI*

The In Between is captivating! It is inspiring and enriching! The combined inner and outer journeys Jenn Baljko shares are intimate and compelling. The nuances she explores in the space between fear and courage helps us appreciate the incredibly rich possibilities we discover when we befriend our emotions. In my many years of work helping others build their emotional literacy, I've not come across a better book to guide the way. I strongly encourage you to immerse yourself in the author's experiences and learning. There is no better companion on your life journey than *The In Between*.

— DAN NEWBY, AUTHOR OF *THE UNOPENED GIFT: A PRIMER IN EMOTIONAL LITERACY* AND *THE FIELD GUIDE TO EMOTIONS*

After walking three and a half years across Asia and Europe, Jennifer Baljko reinvented herself and exchanged fear for courage. *The In Between: Journeying from Fear to Courage* is a decisive and personal guide to overcome deep-rooted fears and march into the world as a fun and fantastic person–without having to walk across two continents.

— BARBARA JENKINS, BESTSELLING AUTHOR OF *SO LONG AS IT'S WILD*

In her book, *The In Between: Journey from Fear to Courage*, she not only gives her readers a taste of what this journey was really like, but she also explores all the emotions that she went through. She gives readers a journaling experience and activities to delve into their emotions. This creates a beautiful woven experience for the reader, connecting them to Jenn's journey and deep emotional spiral path. It is hard to describe what happens to you as the reader. You, too, are transformed, just like Jenn; you experience her complex emotional journey, and you have one of your own. I walked away with more understanding of her two-continent adventures. Although I won't be doing that any time soon, I certainly can relate to and appreciate all the complexities Jenn allows us to explore.

— JESSICA GOLDMUNTZ STOKES, AWARD-WINNING AUTHOR OF *SEEKING CLARITY IN THE LABYRINTH* (NAUTILUS BOOK AWARDS)

The In Between: Journeying from Fear to Courage is like an offering, a road map and guide, viewed through the lens of Jenn's own life challenges. Navigating the narrows between our fears and courage often feels vulnerable and terrifying, yet we manage to navigate them with grace despite our trepidation. Sometimes, bearing witness to someone else's journey and shared wisdom allows us to dig a little deeper into our soul and journey on. Something powerful happens when you realize you have overcome every challenge, using fear and pain not as a limitation but as a catalyst to become the glorious, courageous being you have always been.

— WENDY HUTCHINSON, QUANTUM SOUL HEALER, AUTHOR OF *FINDING THE PATH OF ME*, AND *THE PATH OF ME* PODCAST HOST

It's one thing to understand, intellectually, that the treasure we seek is in the cave we fear. It is quite another thing to run headlong into the terror of uncertainty armed with only boots, a backpack, and a dream. Jenn Baljko's inspirational odyssey extends much farther than the miles she walked between Barcelona and Bangkok. Hers is a journey from gumption to grit to grace, and we readers are invited to follow in her footsteps through practical exercises and journal prompts. If you're ready to claim your treasure, step into the cave with this book as your guiding light.

— ADRIENNE MACIAIN, PH.D., BESTSELLING AUTHOR OF THE *CREATIVE LIVING FOR ALL* SERIES

Ready to explore what fear and fearlessness looks like for you? *The In Between: Journeying from Fear to Courage* is a midlife elixir for women who are ready to look within to excavate their truest, deepest, most authentic selves. Jenn's three year plus, cross-continental journey serves as the backdrop for building courage amid the fear. The truth: It's an inside job. My journey will look nothing like yours. If you're ready to open your heart and mind and see where it leads you on this fear/courage journey, this book is a beautiful and compelling invitation to play and explore what's possible. It can't help but change you in the most empowering and exquisite ways.

— WENDY BATTLES, HOST OF THE *REINVENTION REBELS* PODCAST

A fascinating and useful read. This writer is always thinking of others and how her experiences might be used to make positive change in the world. She shows us that every step of life contains multitudes and the possibility to engage consciously with ourselves and other people.

— URSULA MARTIN, AUTHOR OF *ONE WOMAN WALKS WALES* AND *LONG-DISTANCE WALKER*

JENNIFER BALJKO

THE
IN *between*

JOURNEYING FROM
FEAR TO COURAGE

THE IN BETWEEN
JOURNEYING FROM FEAR TO COURAGE

JENNIFER BALJKO

Red Thread Publishing LLC. 2024

Write to info@redthreadbooks.com if you are interested in publishing with Red Thread Publishing. Learn more about publications or foreign rights acquisitions of our catalog of books: www.redthreadbooks.com

Copyright © 2024 by Jennifer Baljko

All rights reserved.

No part of this book may be reproduced in any form or means. Any unauthorized use, sharing, reproduction or distribution of these materials by any means, electronic, mechanical or otherwise is strictly prohibited. No portion of these materials may be reproduced in any manner whatsoever, without the express written consent of the publisher and the author, except for the use of brief quotations in a book review.

Hardcover ISBN: 979-8-89294-017-7

Paperback ISBN: 979-8-89294-015-3

Ebook ISBN: 979-8-89294-016-0

Cover Design: Red Thread Design

The Emotional Wheel illustration is licensed and used with permission from its artist, Abby VanMuijen (avanmuijen.com).

Other illustrations in the book are the property of the author, Jennifer Baljko, and no part of those illustrations may be used or reproduced without her written permission.

DISCLAIMER

This book is based on true events. It reflects the author's present recollections of experiences over time. Some names, details, and characteristics have been changed; some events have been compressed, and some dialogue has been recreated. The book does not follow the chronological order of the Bangkok Barcelona On Foot walk. Instead, the author has chosen to tell the story by reflecting on different emotional experiences at different moments.

This book and its contents are for informational and educational purposes only. They are not substitutes for medical advice, guidance, or treatment. Topics discussed within the book may cause comfortable and uncomfortable emotions, thoughts, memories, or other sensations. The author acknowledges the complexity of human experiences in this book and advises readers to approach such topics with self-awareness and emotional resilience.

DEDICATION

To anyone who has ever wondered what happens when you face fear but are not quite ready to put on your brave, big-girl panties and charge forward with courage.

CONTENTS

Foreword   xv
Dear Reader   xix

Part I
THE FACADE OF FEARLESSNESS

1. The Woman Who Said Goodbye   3
2. Following the Breadcrumbs   7
3. It Was All So Magical Until It Wasn't   13

Part II
MAPPING FEAR AND COURAGE

4. It's Not a Coin Toss   21
5. Fear as an External Input   25
6. Courage: A Heart-Centered Choice to Act   29
7. A Compass for The In Between   33

Part III
IDENTIFYING EMOTIONAL STEPPING STONES

8. Power to Your Elbow   45
9. I Quit!   53
10. Why Do They Treat Us This Way?   65
11. The Heaviness of Grief   77
12. When You Can't Flee, Negotiate   89
13. Breaking Away From Expectations   103
14. The WOW! Factors   117
15. Drop the Shield You Hide Behind   129

Afterword	135
Thank You	139
Reading Guide	141
Resources to Inspire Your Next Step	147
Acknowledgments	153
Leave a Review	155
About the Author	157
Also by Jennifer Baljko	159
Red Thread Publishing	161

FOREWORD
BY LLUÍS LÓPEZ BAYONA

How would you react if you received an email like this?

> Hi Love,
>   One day in life, before we're old and broken...let's go for a long, long walk...Wouldn't it be cool to walk from Barcelona to Bangkok, or vice versa, for instance? Although Berlin to Barcelona would be easier and shorter...
>   Jenn

I loosened my tie, leaned back in my office chair, and re-read the invitation.

I was astonished...and captivated.

"That's a long, long way," I wrote back, acknowledging the distance between Thailand and Catalonia. I was speechless beyond that sentence.

That June 2013 evening, staring at the world map hanging on our wall, Jenn and I considered our options. It felt like an impossible yet possible idea, something we might be able to do if we just tried, and it came from the amazing and brave woman who wrote this book.

Is this courage? Absurdity? Naivety? A delusion of grandeur?

After more than two years of thinking, digesting, analyzing, and evaluating the pros and cons of a trip of this magnitude, Jenn and I went through a long list of questions we wanted to confront before starting our once-in-a-lifetime experience.

The idea of walking across Asia and Europe for three to five years brought up some of our deepest fears, fears we had never talked about until then. This became our "What if" list of all the worst-case scenarios we could imagine, some of which Jenn shares here.

If we had let our fears win, maybe we would have become frozen or paralyzed, and this walk, one of our most rewarding experiences, never would have happened.

But after many years of traveling separately and together and many other life experiences, we trusted what we both knew: Deep inside ourselves, we have many more resources than we think we have or that we normally use in our comfortable everyday lives. All of us have a limitless amount of resourcefulness we can rely on when we encounter difficult situations.

During the years that our Bangkok Barcelona On Foot walking adventure took place, we inevitably faced a few dangerous and scary situations and several difficult ones. Of course, we did. That is life. Thankfully, we overcame all of them because we trusted ourselves, stayed open to the invitation, and learned how to make good choices between our fears and brave actions.

Jenn's courage and willingness inspired me, her travel buddy and life companion, and many other people we met walking. I hope she inspires you to choose the dream you want to make real.

> – Lluís López Bayona, *author of Àsia i Oceania, Un Any D'Aventura (Asia and Oceania, A Year of Adventure) and long-distance walker*

DEAR READER

Thank you for choosing this book. I want to help you through these pages and encourage you to make easy, empowering choices.

The In Between is a creative nonfiction collection of stories based on situations I lived through and many that I chose to pursue, knowing that they would challenge me in every way physically, mentally, and emotionally.

The book–mostly based on lessons learned from the 16,000-kilometer Bangkok Barcelona On Foot walk I completed in my mid-40s over three-and-a-half years with my life partner Lluís–serves as a starting point for reflections and conversations about fear and courage. Much of the heart-to-heart musing I had between the author's version of me writing this book and the younger version that lived through these experiences centers on how the journey between fear and courage motivated and influenced my choices. I hope that, through my realizations, you begin to notice the patterns and habits you carry into your decision-making process and, with that knowledge, make better and more aligned soul choices.

This kind of inward exploration naturally ushers in a range of emotions, thoughts, and memories, some pleasant and some unpleasant. I'm relying on my expertise as a writing mentor, mindfulness meditation teacher, women's circle facilitator, and intuitive movement/emotional release instructor to guide you in and out of the chapters and through the emotions that may rise and fall as you read them.

The essays and travelogs–the main vehicle for this part-memoir, part-personal development book–contain references to: ancestral lineage trauma, anxiety, death, divorce, grief, hate, heartbreak, immigration, misogyny, rage, regret, shame, stress, supernatural connections, traveling as a couple, traveling as a woman, war, and other topics that may consciously, subconsciously, or unconsciously elicit emotional reactions.

You'll also find stories about love, joy, self-discovery, vulnerability, compassion, and the humanness of living a life filled with flaws, successes, failures, purpose, and meaning. They, too, may stir up something intangible, clarifying, or purifying.

The worksheets in Part III offer contemplations and journaling prompts that may also evoke familiar and unfamiliar, comfortable and uncomfortable feelings, thoughts, or memories. Use the worksheets in a way that satisfies the part of you that wants to study your motives, intentions, choices, and actions when fear and courage are present, or when they are absent.

Dear Reader, you are sovereign. You can choose to put the book down at any moment or continue to journey together. I will be here whenever you are ready for your next step.

Your well-being matters to me. I have tried to be thorough with the content warnings and provided additional details in chapters where content notifications were most relevant and would be most welcomed. I ask for your grace for any warnings that may have been omitted.

With wonder and gratitude,

Jenn

PART I

THE FACADE OF FEARLESSNESS

PART I
THE FACADE OF FEARLESSNESS

~~~~

- How do you know what you know about fear?
- Where did you learn courage, and how has it appeared in your life?
- Could fear and courage be masks you wear to hide other parts of you that you haven't yet learned to express?
- If you looked back over your important choices, how did fear and courage fit into the decision-making process?

I started asking myself these questions when I turned 50. In 2022, the world was in and out of COVID-19 times, its worst moments behind us and the long-term psychological effects still being defined. Three years earlier, I had finished my hardest-ever endeavor, Bangkok Barcelona On Foot, and was unpacking the obvious and subtle lessons I learned from that endurance event. I was also stepping up as a mentor and thought it would be wise to coach myself before I coached others.

Fifty felt like another milestone to study myself again. I wanted to re-learn and understand what motivated me now and what stopped me in my tracks. I wanted to know how I made choices and why I chose what I chose so that I could cross my midlife threshold with grace and take the wisdom I acquired into my crone years. Mostly, I wanted to explore how I navigated fear and courage and what marked the ordinary spaces of life when fear was less present and courage wasn't needed.

The quest into my inner workings brought me back to when my fearlessness skyrocketed. Unraveling a story I told myself for decades revealed something else…a facade I created without knowing it. Here's how the scaffolding went up.

Dear Reader, settle in and begin to wonder and wander back to a time when you felt fearless in your life, career, relationships, and/or choices. Lean into the memory of the courage that made you feel that way. What else do you see from the sacred and safe place of your tender heart?

THE WOMAN WHO SAID GOODBYE

She stands on the porch of her childhood home, forlorn and uncertain, ready and eager.

Her father puts her gigantic blue backpack and the smaller trolley luggage, packed with stuff that comforts her soul, into the Jeep's back seat. She justifies needing all of it...the short black skirt, the fancy silk blouse, two bikinis, a stack of notebooks, multi-colored pens, three pairs of shoes, and several travel guidebooks. She will learn later what is truly essential. Right now, everything feels important.

She holds back the tears her mother is already crying. Rays of spring sunshine twinkle in her mother's eyes, glistening with affection and understanding.

"I hope you find what you're looking for," her mother says, pulling her daughter into a hug only a mom can give.

"Me, too," whispers the 31-year-old woman, holding her mother a little tighter and wishing herself easier days ahead. The wonder of it all–the what-could-have-been scenarios, the broken promises of a broken relationship, the unknowable possibilities that might unfold–is sometimes overwhelming.

But the choice to say goodbye and start again was made nine

months earlier in September 2002, and she's determined to stick with this decision.

Soon after filing for divorce and ending 12 years of couplehood that started during her freshman year in college, the woman heard that familiar voice from somewhere deep inside her heart...the one that always knows more than her intellect does, the one that challenges her not to give up...the one that provides direction in difficult times.

"Stop feeling sorry for yourself. Your marriage is over. Save your money. Quit your job. Travel solo around Southern Europe. Make it an adventure," the voice said with absolute clarity and unquestionable resolve.

The woman had trusted this voice before at various other milestones requiring hard choices, pivots into uncharted, rough waters, and tenacious actions.

"What are you saying?" the woman ventured to ask, already knowing intuitively that any answer would cause a domino effect of new, unexpected decisions waiting for her.

The voice laughed. *"You know what I'm saying. You have to make a choice. What I'm offering you is an invitation to make your soul happy. Will you take it?"*

It was an all-is-lost-and-something-has-to-change Eat, Pray, Love moment three and a half years before Elizabeth Gilbert published her best-selling memoir, which inspired and forever changed the course of millions of women's lives.

The woman barely noticed her fear and instead did what she always did: armored up with courage and said *HELL, YES!* to life's dare. If she had been truly honest with herself, she would have seen the emotional undercurrent of this particular HELL, YES! was a hard-headed righteousness that rang with the pluckiness of *"You don't want to build a life with me, screw it! I'll show you what I can do! Just you watch!"*

Months later, standing on the porch with her mother on a bright May day in 2003, the woman could not possibly know how this trip, this single choice to go, would reshape every thought she ever had about freedom, independence, and confidence. She cannot yet imagine the friends she would connect with, the things she would learn about herself, the insecurities that would make her weep, or the love she would feel for and from a man who happened to be in a crowded square in Barcelona and who, after their chance meeting, would hold her and her heart with great tenderness well into her 50s.

The only thing this woman knows at this moment is that it's time to leave behind what was and find a way to welcome whatever will come next. She knows that a journey of a million steps starts with choosing to take the first step in any direction, so she takes that step.

The woman smiles at her mother. She walks down the stairs and into a new life with no form or familiarity.

She tunes into her heart full of courage as she waves goodbye.

She hears a distant call, *"Ready, Set...Go!"*

She leaps without a net.

FOLLOWING THE BREADCRUMBS

Y ou guessed it! That 31-year-old woman standing on the porch is me…twenty-one years younger than I am now.

That first solo backpacking trip, a wanderlust-infused disconnect from life as I knew it, was one of the many breadcrumbs I chose to follow, and it influenced many other choices decades later.

WHO WAS THAT WOMAN?

How did I know to listen to and trust that inner voice?

How did I muster up enough courage and confidence to quit my good-paying journalism job and travel to faraway places for an extended amount of time with barely enough money in my bank account to get by?

How did I deal with the fear, worry, doubt, inexperience, and innocence of flinging myself out into the world without directions or instructions?

How did I nurture the joy, curiosity, and willingness to explore this other self I was creating and molding?

Thinking back to that time, it dawns on me that my answers are uninspiring. The shortest answer is that I was in my 30s and felt I had everything to gain from that choice of traveling solo.

The only reasons I can remember for doing what I did, which in the early 2000s sounded unreasonable to many people I told, were:

- Life sucked for a while when I was getting divorced from my college sweetheart.
- I felt like a failure and wanted to run away.
- I thought I could be someone else for a while, and traveling to places where no one knew me allowed me to experiment with who I wanted to be without other people's expectations and disappointments.
- Wandering the world seemed to be a better choice than drowning my sadness with midnight binges of mint chocolate chip ice cream (That felt good only one night).

It felt so good to do what I did on the solo trip, to create a more empowered version of myself, to come back with the reward of making it on my own. Yet, something, a wish, a desire, a longing, remained unanswered, unfulfilled, and unsatisfied...as if my quest to know myself had only just begun.

Did your *Eat, Pray, Love* trip feel like that, too? Like you finally had permission to wild yourself after years of staying the course other people had defined for you, and you could be any kind of brave you wanted to be. Yet some other deeper soul-calling remained unanswered and needed more time and self-study.

For many years after that trip, I told people it was the most fearless I had ever felt. But, what recently revealed itself to me during one of the drafts of this book is that back in my 30s, I felt so fearless because I didn't know how to be afraid. I didn't know how to recognize or name my fears and insecurities. I didn't have any EQ (emotional quotient) training in my younger years because emotions didn't seem to matter much where I came from. My intellect, not my emotions, would advance my studies, career, and life. I learned that, if I let them, emotions would get in the way of my success, and success mattered the most to me in my formative years.

Maybe you got this message, too. What I absorbed consciously or unconsciously from my family, the culture in the United States, and my neighborhood in the 1970s, 80s, and 90s was that there was no time or tolerance for fear.

Crying was a flaw. Vulnerability was a weakness. Being scared was a hindrance. In my small corner of the world in New Jersey, showing anything that resembled fear put me at risk of being humiliated and teased; I already had a bad run through that with braces and glasses by my 10th birthday, so no way was fear going to bully me.

I understood that courage was the antidote to anything that sparked a fear impulse. Courage, in whatever way it showed up, was rewarded, especially if it helped me become a better student, productive adult, and Wonder Woman-do-it-all kind of wife, mother, and employee. My way through life was to be tough, armored up, with my big-girl panties on. I was supposed to be ready and willing to jump towards any next big thing with boldness, bravery, or bravado.

In those "I'll show you" years up to my mid-30s, I strived for the ordinary things dangled in front of me–good grades, a good university, a good company with good pay, and a good marriage with a good family life. The courage I needed to obtain that status matched accordingly: I took measured risks that raised eyebrows and stretched my wings beyond my perceived comfort zone. The secret I never told anyone is that I always knew the limit of how brave or bold I wanted to be. I would go as far as I could go until I felt my safety was jeopardized.

Going off to experience the world alone, on my own terms, stirred something in me. Long before the digital nomad lifestyle became a trend, I remember thinking on the plane to Athens, my first stop on the solo six-month adventure, *"What if I really like traveling like this? What if I like living in different places for a while and don't want to return to how things were?"*

In this context, cutting cords and saying goodbye to a past that was over felt fairly normal in my 30-something skin, so much so that I didn't know how courageous I was until people told me I was courageous. I thought it was just another step forward that had to be taken, so I ignored whatever other emotions may have been there (and may have stopped me) and forged on blindly to my ideal future.

Without being aware of it, my go-to courage remedy for all of life's ills solidified into a complex facade of fearlessness. It was a mask I wore without knowing it was a mask.

Each time my courage was applauded, another layer of scaffolding went up on my fearlessness facade. I grew comfortable with being the odd one out, the fearless one (or was it the foolish one?), the intrepid one who could do–and wanted to prove that I could do–hard things. I ran up every personal and professional mountain with a shield of courage and a razor-sharp machete to win, succeed, and show the world I was a worthy human.

Whatever life tossed my way, I stood ready in fight mode, believing that a fierce, full-body, full-mind act of courage was the only thing I needed to go the distance. This was the foundation I built most of my life on until my 40s. It was an invented structure that held everything together.

HOW A 16,0000-KILOMETER WALK MADE SENSE TO ME

The accumulation of courage I experienced in the earlier half of my life led me towards one of my most important choices and my most significant accomplishment: A three-and-a-half-year walk across Asia and Europe.

With the choice to do this walk and the ongoing choice to keep learning from it years after we crossed the finish line, a scattering of new crumbs caught my attention and, one by one, began to show me what I had ignored most of life: The dozens of emotions that bubbled up in response to fears I skipped over with courage.

The gathering of these morsels through the entire decade of my 40s and into the first years of my 50s continues to help me deconstruct my fearlessness facade. They help me show up with more authenticity, which, in turn, ironically, makes me more authentically fearless as I step forward with a heart of courage.

In essence, as I write this book, I am tearing down the old way I used to walk in the world and wondering about the other emotions that shape the liminal space between fear and courage.

Looking back through life's rearview mirror (which you'll be invited to do, too, in the worksheets coming up later in the book), the backpacking trip I did in my 30s, more than any other accomplishment, gave me the confidence I needed to say HELL, YES! to what life dared me to do a decade later when I was 41 years old.

The familiar voice that knows more than my intellect and intuitively nudges me in soul-led directions teased me again in June 2013 with this single sentence: Before you're old and broken, go for a long, long walk…like across two continents.

At that moment, all my inner fear-based bells, whistles, and alarms should have glared warnings at me about the ridiculousness of such an odyssey. Instead, the invitation's allure filled me with awe, curiosity, and fascination. In a split second, my imagination ran wild and started showing me infinite possibilities that could come from accepting a challenge like this.

Walk two continents??? What…something like Asia and Europe? Could I really do something like that???

My mind spun the movie reel of me walking the Earth, and my next thought without much hesitation was, *"Could I convince someone else to say HELL, YES! and walk with me??? Hmmm… would HE do this with me?"*

The person who gave his stamp of approval and upped our lives' ante within a few hours of hearing the early version of what would become our <u>Bangkok Barcelona On Foot</u> walk is Lluís, the man I fell in love with in a crowded square in Barcelona ten years earlier and was willing to change my life for…he's the man who still holds me and my heart with tenderness. My love and life partner (who wrote the book's foreword) also found this breadcrumb intriguing.

While the proposal to uproot our lives and walk for three, four, maybe even five years lit up his wanderlust-filled backpacker heart, other things assured the YES! from both of us.

The combination of wanting to shake up the routine of our comfortable everyday life alongside the once-in-a-lifetime challenge to try something extraordinary like walking two continents moved the needle for us.

It was HELL, YES! because we felt strong in our minds, bodies, and hearts.

It was HELL, YES! because it sounded like an experience that would make our lives memorable, something we would cherish forever because we had tried to do it.

It was HELL, YES! because we felt fearless… until we didn't.

IT WAS ALL SO MAGICAL UNTIL IT WASN'T

EMOTIONAL WELL-BEING WARNING:

> This chapter mentions the threat of potential violence, sexual assault, death, and other situations that may cause panic or worry.

"Can we talk about the hard things we may face?" I asked Lluís one day while walking in our favorite Barcelona park.

"Of course. What's on your mind?" he said.

"The big fears," I said, dreading what I would say next.

In the months leading up to our January 2016 flight to Bangkok to start our walk home to Barcelona (see our walking map in the "Resources to Inspire Your Next Step" section at the end of the book), fear and all the insecurities that come with fear slowly began to chip away at my confidence.

One moment, I fluttered excitedly about the places we would pass through and the people we would meet. We were so convinced about the higher purpose of the walk that we gave it a subtitle, "Exploring the world, seeking the goodness of people." Lluís and I constantly talked about the kindness we hoped to find in many places. (In fact, we found so much kindness, we have a documentary film about it that was screened at eight international film festivals and is the topic of many of our recent walk-related presentations).

In another moment, while reviewing our planned route through vast expanses of Asia and Europe and 21 nation-states with languages we didn't speak, I questioned if I was physically, mentally, and emotionally prepared to handle the unknown and inevitable difficulties that would come with such a grandiose undertaking. I grew suspicious about how people would treat us as strangers in their countries and speculated if we would become victims in other people's stories. I doubted myself and my ability to stay courageous for the long haul. I second-guessed my intuition about this choice, and that was a surprising first for me.

The choice to do this big walk in my 40s triggered a 180-degree shift from where I was in my 30s. Rather than feeling I had everything to gain from this adventure, the pit in my stomach showed me how quickly I could lose everything I loved and lived for.

"What will we do if we are kidnapped? What if we're taken hostage? What if I'm raped? What if you're raped? What if people target their hate at us? What if we're bitten by a poisonous snake or mauled by a bear? What if one of us dies?" Every fear I had the courage to think about surged through me and out of my mouth. I couldn't hold back all the scary thoughts anymore. Too many terrifying news headlines got the best of me, and I flinched.

Before panic set in, Lluís guided me to a park bench.

He told me about the fear-filling What-if scenarios causing him to worry. Topping his list were being arrested for misunderstanding geopolitical issues, having trouble getting the visas we required for each country, preventing bacterial and viral infections that could destroy our health, leaving his aging parents alone, and the fatal possibility of treating a ruptured appendix in a remote place without a nearby hospital.

We spent a few hours listing the worst-case dangers causing us anxiety and apprehension. The simple naming of our fears made them feel less imminent and threatening, and from that calmer state of mind, we played with concepts that felt like potential solutions to would-be worries. Even though our travel and life experiences reminded us that we would not know how we would react in those situations until they happened, we comforted each other with workable A-B-C options that could spring into action if needed. We identified practical things we could do to help dismantle our initial fears and created safety parameters to temporarily pacify us.

"Each family will have copies of our passports and insurance documents. We will keep our emergency contact information with our passports. We'll use Instagram and email to let our families generally know where we are en route," Lluís said, showing me how small details could mitigate the panic I was beginning to feel about our walk.

As Lluís and I deconstructed a few What-if scenarios, I imagined another way of approaching fear and courage. It appeared in my mind's eye as a map through a spiral path of the emotions I was finally ready to see, feel, and use to make better choices.

PART II

MAPPING FEAR AND COURAGE

PART II
MAPPING FEAR AND COURAGE

- What if the assumption that there is a straight line between fear and courage was wrong?
- If you mapped it as a walk through life, what could a journey from fear to courage look like?
- What else shows up between fear and courage, and how could you use those emotions to empower yourself?
- How would you navigate new fork-in-the-road choice points if the high-voltage charge around fear and courage softened and the decision-making process felt easeful?

With the facade of fearlessness that marked my 30s falling away, the truth of what I thought I knew about fear and courage shifted, too. And that meant experimenting with the boundaries of my emotional intelligence and being willing to change my perspective about what I thought I knew.

Life is funny and fun that way, isn't it? Just when you think you know what you're doing and how you would respond to whatever life tosses you, a fresh set of circumstances forces you to recalculate your route and steer towards alternative and unfamiliar destinations.

Throughout the Bangkok Barcelona On Foot walk, my emotional compass changed daily, and I'll show how later in Part III. However, what keeps coming back to me is how, in my mind's eye, the emotional wheel commonly employed today in conversations about healthy emotional expression overlapped with a labyrinth-like spiral path, one of my favorite shapes and symbols. That's the ground we'll stand on in this section as we survey our inner landscape and chart what lies between fear and courage.

Dear Reader, envision a spiral path that curves between your fear impulses and the courageous actions you choose to take. As you step forward, consider what other emotions you may have felt when fear and courage start mingling on your life's dance floor.

IT'S NOT A COIN TOSS

I get confused by how people–how I–compare things and what is compared. Comparing fear and courage as a coin toss, for example, spins my mind upside down. It pulled me into a rabbit hole while outlining this book.

I'm not sure how I picked up this image–perhaps it's rooted in my own courage-as-a-shield-to-fear response or how the personal growth and wellness communities talk about it–but I often visualized fear and courage as two sides of the same coin.

I thought it was easy to switch off fear and turn on courage. Flip a coin and you may have your head full of fear. Flip the coin again and you may have the strong tail of courage, perhaps something a dragon would use to protect its treasure and fight off a thief entering its lair.

Many friends my age hold some of these same preconceived notions. We used to call it ambition, and we still do.

We are Generation X, the women who stood on the shoulders of the women before us who pioneered civil rights movements that ensured equal rights for women and all humans. Taking our generational turn was, and maybe still is, our responsibility to break the glass ceilings, confidently shake up male-dominated industries, and take our place as leaders at the table so that the women who come after us and stand on our shoulders can lift society higher.

Courage, in all its forms, was a non-negotiable asset we had to figure out how to use and manipulate to compete with the boys and men who dictated our professional promotions and decided if and how we rose through the ranks. Getting through those battles certainly scarred us, and they probably scared us, too. But at least for a short while, we felt accomplished, fulfilled, and satisfied…until we didn't.

In frequent conversations I now have with midlife women and older sages, the crones among us, who achieved most of the goals they set for themselves, I see how they shrug their shoulders and wonder, *"What now? Is that it? I'm the boss with multiple degrees, divorced with kids, a nice house, a nice car, doing half marathons and Ironmans for fun, volunteering with community organizations, and traveling where and when I want. What other goodness can I dream up and manifest?"*

That's the place of discomfort for many of us–me, you, and other women like us: Feeling like we have achieved enough and have too much to lose when life, circumstances, and soul-calling dreams yank us in new directions. The fear of failure, rejection, and a crash-and-burn landing hold us back and keep us contained or constrained to the life we already built.

But thanks to women such as Brené Brown, a world-renowned researcher, we have tools and an expanded vocabulary to reinvent how we express ourselves and our emotions. Brown's concept that we can be both courageous AND vulnerable is revolutionary to me. It is the wrecking ball I'm hurling into the fearlessness facade I walled myself behind for too long.

Each year that passes, I see how my assumption that courage is the straight-line reaction to fear was wrong, or at least not fully accurate. My longtime notion that I had to be fearful or fearless, cowardly or courageous, and that almost nothing else existed between those extremes, is crumbling one day at a time.

I once believed courage alchemized fear. Now, I wonder, is the truer alchemizing agent something in between fear and courage? Is courage what bubbles up after lead was turned to gold, and because some other unnamed substance triggered the transformation before we actually saw or appreciated the full effect of the change? Is something else responsible for altering fear into courage?

I realize now it is not a coin toss, where I'm one way of being or another at any given moment. It is not a short, straight line between fear and courage. It is a winding journey through many emotions, mindsets, and states of being. Life also brings me disappointment, disillusionment, anger, frustration, sadness, joy, compassion, empathy, equanimity, and dozens of other feelings, and those states of being affect how I filter fear impulses, cultivate courage, and choose what I choose.

So my model is changing, my understanding is shifting, and this is how it's taking form.

FEAR AS AN EXTERNAL INPUT

Let's start first with clarifying words around fear.

In our context, and consolidated from various sources listed in the resources section at the end of this book, fear is a primal and universally recognized feeling that surfaces when there is an external threat or danger to our physical, emotional, or psychological safety.

Fear is a survival mechanism that keeps us out of harm's way. When we face a real or perceived threat, our bodies experience biochemical changes often expressed as fight, flight, freeze, and fawn responses.

Fear shows itself in many ways, with different intensities and reactions. Sometimes fear is in plain sight. Sometimes you may need a microscope to find it tucked under a host of other feelings, including, for instance, insecurity, anxiety, worry, dread, panic, or despair, to name a few.

In my life, fear doesn't frequently come with a flashing neon sign that says, "Hello! Here I am. I'm fear." Since I've hidden myself behind fearlessness for so long, I usually have to excavate an array of feelings, such as anger, anxiety, guilt, and righteousness, before I understand the possible connection to fear. I have chosen to dissect a handful of emotional walk-related moments as examples of how I move through the initial sparks that feel like fear, things I call fear impulses, and eventually take a courageous next step.

Fear impulses may appear as bodily sensations, like the hairs standing up on the back of your neck or a gut feeling that something is off. They may also come in as thoughts, questions, or harsh comments trying to make logical sense of something happening around you. For example, as your body perceives and processes these initial fear signals, your mind might ask: What happened here? Am I safe? What is this bodily response I'm having? What should I do now?

I'm learning to pay more attention to the early signs of fear and how my common versions of fear grab and hold my attention. Because if I can discern earlier what flares up my anger, righteousness, or other triggering emotions, I can pause, take a breath, and notice something like this instead, "Oh, this is the part of me that wants to fight to be right." Then with that new awareness, I can come to my choice point with more heart-centered emotional information and the question "Is this worth fighting for?," and avoid lunging impulsively into a scrimmage.

IS IT FEAR? OR IS IT AN INSECURITY?

It's important to make another distinction when we talk about fear. In Western countries, we tend to toss all our uncomfortable emotions under the same umbrella and call everything a fear.

But, if we filter fear through the above definition of being a real or perceived threat or danger to our safety, what should we call the feelings that chip away at our confidence and self-esteem? The things that don't present any imminent, threatening danger yet consume our energy with feelings of inadequacy, negative self-talk, and low self-worth?

Those feelings are better described as insecurities.

As we study our patterns of fear and courage and examine the spaces in between them as an intermediary journey, we may discover that what we usually want to name a fear could be reframed as insecurity.

In my mind, insecurities are easier to deal with. Take my fear of failure, for example. I don't feel that failure in my everyday work or life is a physical threat so big that I would be harmed significantly if I fell short. My insecurity around failure, however, is that I don't like setbacks, wasted effort, or mistakes. My insecurity heightens when I am people-pleasing and strive for perfection. Those qualities are very different from an external input that may be fatal or unsafe.

My dare to you, dear reader, is to challenge yourself to think beyond what has become common vernacular for fear and reflect on what is true for you. Ask yourself repeatedly: Is this fear I'm feeling or insecurity? How do they feel and act similarly or differently? How do I respond to them?

COURAGE: A HEART-CENTERED CHOICE TO ACT

I'll be the first to lay down the shield of courage I have used for years to push every river of fear I had to cross. It's essential to my growth and expansion into wiser crone years (and I hope you are nodding with me) that I appreciate courage as something other than a life force wrapped up with ambitious striving and proving my worth.

To up-level my knowledge of courage, I first turned to the Merriam-Webster Dictionary definition: "Courage is the mental or moral strength to venture, persevere, and withstand danger, fear, or difficulty."

Moral strength. Venture. Persevere. My 31-year-old self likes these words–a lot.

Through this lens, we can see how courage was condensed into phrases many of us grew up with:

> *Be brave.*
> *Do it scared.*
> *Fortune favors the bold.*
> *Take the bull by the horns.*
> *Never give up.*

Courage is mastering fear, not the absence of fear.
Put on your big-girl panties, and suck it up.

The Greek philosopher Plato gave wings to the dictionary definition with the following quote: "Courage is knowing what not to fear."

"Hmmm...that feels like courage's basic responsibility. Courage's job should be figuring out what to worry about and what not to worry about. It took us three-and-a-half years of walking to learn that, remember?" my not-so-long-ago-47-year-old self chimes in with a sarcastic eye roll.

Yes, I do remember, all too well. During Bangkok Barcelona On Foot, Lluís and I became unexpected experts at distinguishing which big or small fears, ours and other people's, might escalate to panic and what tizzy could be dissolved with tenderness.

Courage, however, involves more than the mind's moral tenets. We discover this when we layer its Latin roots from the word cor, or heart.

I like how Brené Brown–the previously mentioned author, professor, and researcher known for her work on courage, empathy, shame, and vulnerability–talks about it: "In one of its earliest forms, the word courage had a very different definition than it does today. Courage originally meant 'To speak one's mind by telling all one's heart.'"

This last bit–to speak one's mind by telling all one's heart–is my 52-year-old's current emotional baseline for examining courage. Let's also make it our collective starting point for the rest of the book.

Our hearts speak in many ways, and so does our courage. If courage is a way our hearts talk to us and also provides the mental and moral strength we need to face danger and difficulty, then it's easier to recognize courage in its many forms. Courage is boldness, bravery, determination, fortitude, resilience, and tenacity. And, yes, in many situations, courage is calmness, empathy, equanimity, inner peace, and patience, among other things.

The best part is that, if we're aware of it, we get to choose every moment of every day what big-girl panties we hoist up and march out into the world with.

What do you say? Shall we shop around for the courage panties that better fit us now?

A COMPASS FOR THE IN BETWEEN

~~~

Mapping an emotional journey between fear and courage is tricky. I am illustrating abstractions that may weather over time, the same way my physical, mental, and emotional bodies wither and change. What I thought I knew about fear and courage has shifted every decade I've lived, as it should, and it will certainly shift many more times as I age. We have to continuously, and willingly, unshackle ourselves from ideas we locked into our minds and hearts; those old ideas take us far, and then new ideas take us further.

Maybe you'll come up with something better; maybe I will. This work-in-progress theory will evolve. But for now, for this book, I humbly offer you the map I'm using to journey from fear to courage in my everyday life. It's something I unwittingly seeded during the Bangkok Barcelona On Foot walk when time slowed to a pace of three kilometers an hour, and something that took root in 2023 while bringing the collaborative book *Fierce Awakenings* to life.

Before we examine the model, ground in with these concepts.

The first assumption we have to make is that there is a journey worth navigating between fear and courage.

Our starting point is that we don't simply flip a coin and instantly become afraid or courageous. That may happen sometimes in urgent life-or-death decision-making situations. But, really, the journey is the acknowledgment that many other emotions, feelings, thoughts, and perceptions influence, impact, and inform how we manage fear and act with courage.

Understanding how we usually respond to a fear impulse and noting what other emotions fill the gap after the initial fear impulse subsides eases the pressure of having to respond courageously every single time. Responding courageously to everything life hits us with can be exhausting and, perhaps even, frustrating and dissatisfying as we seek a quick-fix solution or embody a fleeting feeling of success.

Marking the slower journey through many other emotions provides valuable, and lasting, information we can use to make better choices. In making better choices, we align more authentically with our soul's calling and wisely prepare ourselves to answer that call first with a genuine and audacious HELL, YES! and then with appropriate actions.

The second assumption is that each person's journey will be different, and our own individual journeys change constantly.

Every one of us feels, embodies, and expresses fear differently at different moments of life. Every person's journey from fear to courage includes an uncountable number of emotional combinations that are constantly changing. What felt brave in our 20s or 30s might cause worry in our 50s or distress in our 70s. Or vice versa. What we shied away from as young adults may make us adventurous and gutsy crones.

Our map must remain adaptable to best respond to changing emotional needs while helping us recognize the patterns we default to over time.

The last assumption is that mixing models and overlapping concepts is okay to receive more clarity.

My experience as a participant in and facilitator of women's circles is that we face limitations in interpreting and vocalizing the intangible feelings our bodies know as vibrational or sensory-based languages. For instance, how do you describe, in words, a gut feeling?

Even though I like clear processes and models to describe things, individual blueprints sometimes fall short and don't show a complete picture. By overlapping two concepts, my view has widened and I can better describe what lies between my fear and my courage.

The journeying map I created and now present here is a blend of an emotional wheel and the sacred symbol of a labyrinth-like spiral path.

Therapists, counselors, and personal development coaches use emotional wheels, also called a wheel of emotions, to help clients expand their emotional literacy, improve their emotional awareness, express the intensity of the emotional experience, and provide tools for emotional regulation.

Emotional wheels look like this one, licensed and used with permission from Artist Abby VanMuijen (avanmuijen.com).

Art by Abby VanMuijen
avanmuijen.com
Used with persimmission from the artist

Using the emotional wheel in conjunction with a spiral-shaped path leading inwards to the center gives us another layer of depth and connection to our emotional well-being and expression.

Observing my life's journey as a spiral pulling me inwards, outwards, and upwards, rather than as a Point A to Point B linear experience took on greater meaning for me in 2023. While leading 12 women (11 others and myself) through the nine-month creation of a collaborative book, *Fierce Awakenings: Calling in Courage and Confidence to Walk Life's Spiral Path*, published by the same company publishing this book, Red Thread Publishing LLC, the stepping stones between fear and courage began to reveal themselves.

In that book, we each wrote a chapter reflecting how courage moved us through adversity, loss, and personal reinvention to greater self-trust, confidence, and freedom. The deeper work involved lovingly shepherding each of these women through their fears about raising their once-stifled voices, sharing their vulnerabilities, and owning their stories.

Our monthly writers' circles ebbed and flowed through nervousness, anxiety, excitement, joy, pride, and achievement, and mirrored what I witnessed in other groups. I had an inside view into the inner workings of how women came to the same gathering with very similar and very different approaches to living with fear and courage and how they went back out into the world with confidence or something like it.

In this new book, I take the spiral path idea and turn it into a labyrinth leading to the emotional engine of our hearts. We walk into the labyrinth with a known fear or an external impulse we sense or recognize as fear. As we keep stepping forward, many other emotions appear as stepping stones, and the invitation is to pause and explore what that particular emotion feels like.

We keep rounding the curves, acknowledging different emotions, until we arrive at the grounded heart of courage, where we choose, cultivate, and nurture a brave or bold action. From a state of being in courage, we step back out into the world, ready to meet other emotions in a new way…until we encounter another fear, and the cycle begins again.

We go in and out of the spiral, sometimes with the same patterns of emotions accompanying us and sometimes with completely different ones marking our journey. Each time, we elevate the intimate knowing of who we are, what masks we hide behind, and what facades we can bulldoze.

In its simplest view, it looks like this. Here, I mention emotions I frequently encounter as I journey from fear to courage, and use them as the labyrinth's stepping stones.

THIS IS *THE IN BETWEEN* COMPASS.

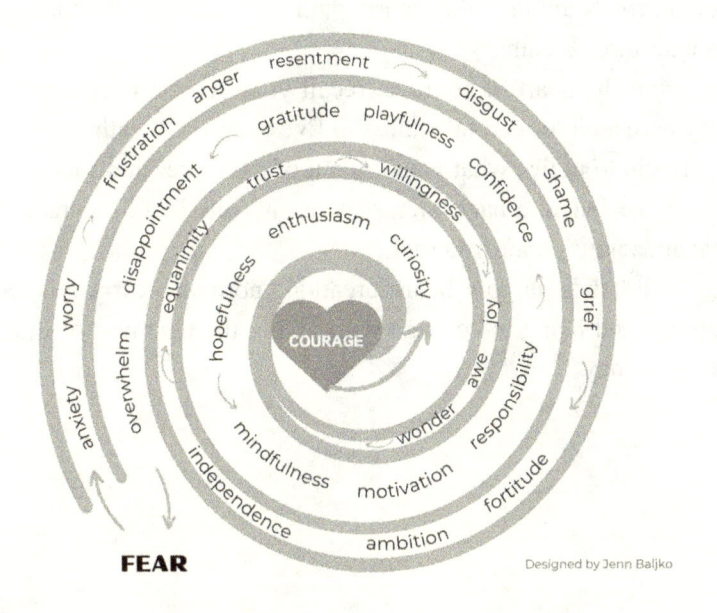

[Spiral diagram from FEAR to COURAGE with emotions: anxiety, worry, overwhelm, disappointment, frustration, anger, resentment, disgust, shame, grief, responsibility, fortitude, ambition, motivation, independence, mindfulness, hopefulness, equanimity, trust, gratitude, enthusiasm, playfulness, willingness, confidence, curiosity, joy, awe, wonder — Designed by Jenn Baljko]

☉ WORKSHEET: WADE IN WITH WONDER

Imagine walking into the labyrinth-like spiral path with the blank compass below.

Review the emotional wheel and the spiral illustration provided.

Take a comfortable seat. Inhale and exhale for three cycles of breath. Notice and name what feels present, and be with that emotion for three more breath cycles.

Remember a time you felt afraid? Mark that on the spiral path as your fear impulse. Take three cycles of breath.

Using the emotional wheel as a vocabulary nudge, try to remember what other emotions may have been present. Fill in the spiral with as many emotions, thoughts, and states of being as you can remember as you keep "walking" the spiral path to the heart of courage. Take another three breaths.

From the heart of courage, recall your actions in response to fear. Stay here a bit longer; take three to five cycles of breath.

Begin to notice what walking out of the center in a state of courage may have felt like back then or what it feels like now, remembering that audacious action you took.

With hands on your heart, breathing normally, carry this feeling of courage and being in courage with you in the next part of the book or into your day.

A COMPASS FOR THE IN BETWEEN

Art by Abby VanMuijen
avanmuijen.com
Used with persimission from the artist

THE IN BETWEEN

FEAR → COURAGE

Designed by Jenn Baljko

PART III

IDENTIFYING EMOTIONAL STEPPING STONES

PART III
IDENTIFYING EMOTIONAL STEPPING STONES

- How do you discern small fears from big ones and not make mountains out of molehills?
- As Plato suggests, how can you use courage as a barometer to know what not to fear?
- How do you know whether to fight, flee, freeze, or fawn in the face of fear?
- When does your courage need to be loud? When can it be quiet?

Here's where we lace up our boots, walk with fear and courage, and practice noticing the in between emotions waiting to be discovered.

I selected seven moments from Bangkok Barcelona On Foot to show some of my lessons and how I learned them. Appropriately, the first essay comes from a Persian phrase meaning "Don't be tired," a good starting point for the lifetime journey of recognizing the spaces between fear and courage.

When talking about Bangkok Barcelona On Foot, I often say this was the longest walk I ever took to reach the home of my heart. My wish is to save you three and a half years of blisters and back pain, and hand this experience to you in the form of personal essays and worksheets. The journaling prompts, I hope, will inspire you to wade into the emotional exploration process with wonder, help you deconstruct fear-based myths, and discover new ways to navigate your inner landscape.

Dear Reader, we are now on The In Between spiral path. The following essays do not follow the chronological order of the walk. If you want to know more about the linear journey, there's a map of our route in the resources section at the back of the book, or you can visit bangkokbarcelonaonfoot.com and read our blog. Here, we bend time and place, and follow emotional ebbs and flows, which have their own clocks.

For the globetrotters among us, I have added the location of each essay to spark wanderlust. Even if you never ever consider doing a walk like I did and never ever step foot in the countries I write about, I'm trusting the divine inspiration that helped me select these particular moments from the thousands of possible options to thread a common experience through some core emotions that make us all human. Have your walking stick? Ok, let's go!

P.S. I have also included emotional well-being warnings, when relevant, so you can choose when to rest your mind and heart and when to join the hike again. I'm also listing the fear impulses and courageous actions as mile markers you can watch out for as you walk through the essay.

POWER TO YOUR ELBOW

―〜―

EMOTIONAL WELL-BEING WARNING:

> Finding pleasant surprises in a place negatively portrayed by many people and news organizations.

LOCATION: IRAN

FEAR IMPULSES:

- *Why do I still feel so unprepared?*
- *What are these people saying to me? I don't understand them. Can I trust them?*
- *Can I quit this hard thing? Who cares if I finish?*

WHAT'S IN THE IN BETWEEN SPACE?

- *Curiosity*

- *Boredom*
- *Exhaustion*
- *Kindness*
- *Inspiration*
- *Motivation*
- *Optimism*
- *Eagerness*
- *Joy*
- *Victory*

COURAGEOUS RESPONSES:

- *Savoring the small details of every day*
- *Appreciating the kindness others offer you*
- *Returning kindness with a smile and a thank you*

Wherever we walked, we were strangers in strange lands. Lluís and I knew early on that we would have to be comfortable with people suspiciously staring at us as we did our thing in life. We were on their turf, and we looked weird.

Simultaneously, we had to learn to trust others and discern when something felt unsafe. To do that, we needed to trust our intuition even more than we already did. So, we tuned in more to what was happening around us, to people's body language, to the tone of their voices, and to the warmth of their smiles.

In Iran, a country often depicted as the world's enemy, we found incredible kindness in ways we never felt elsewhere. But it was in the frequency of their simple wish, "*Khaste nabashid*! Power to your Elbow. Don't be tired," that I found the strength to walk thousands of miles forward.

POWER TO YOUR ELBOW

Khaste nabashid!

For weeks, these words follow us.

They float off the lips of most Iranians who notice Lluís and me walking through their towns, our big backpacks weighing us down. Power to your elbow, they say, with a victorious fist pump.

During our two months of traipsing along the Caspian Sea, strangers–and strangers who became friends when they invited us to share a tea–wished us this nicety: *Salam*, hello. *Khaste nabashid*!

I chuckle and return the greeting with a smile and the Persian/Farsi word for thank you, *sepas*.

Faced with the daily, arduous task of walking across two continents from Bangkok, Thailand, to Barcelona, Catalonia, my feet, hips, and back need far more power than my elbows. But I deeply appreciate everyone who takes a minute to cheer us on. Their kindness in noticing our Herculean effort to move through life at the slow pace of three kilometers an hour lifts my heart.

When I ask people what the saying means to them, they tilt their heads sideways and shrug, translating the Farsi into English, saying, "Don't be tired."

I see why they say that to us. Lluís, my life and walking partner, and I look tired because we are tired. We walk 25 to 30 kilometers most days, carrying, on average, 20 kilograms. By the time we cross Iran, the geographical midpoint of our 16,000-kilometer adventure, we have come far, AND we still have so much further to go.

Khaste nabashid! Power to your elbow. Don't be tired. Thank you/*sepas*. This becomes a familiar greeting through cities and rural areas, a comfortable space between footsteps, an encouraging boost to persevere when it is so hard to do that.

For kilometers and kilometers, and weeks and weeks, I mull over this phrase. I listen closer to how people say it…how their faces light up when they bless us with this wish…how they hug us with these words when we finish our tea… how we all get teary-eyed when it's time to say goodbye and plod on.

With *khaste nabashid* rolling around my heart and "power to my elbow" becoming a mantra during the toughest moments of the day when I could use more courage, I see a flurry of magical dots connect themselves, and I learn something new. From somewhere inside me, I hear, *"Ohhhhh...Don't be tired; it's just the beginning!"*

The more I hear this adage and walk with it, the more I interpret and understand what isn't being said.

I feel into the wishes they bestow upon us that transcend words, language, and culture. They melt any fear about continuing to do this really hard thing and strengthen my resolve to walk homeward through unconventional places.

The next time I hear *khaste nabashid!* I translate it to:

> *Good luck!*
> *May your endeavor be successful.*
> *May you stay strong in mind, body, and heart as life*
>   *calls to you.*
> *Go...keep greeting life.*
> *Choose to walk on.*
> *Keep saying YES! to the invitations that rise up*
>   *before you.*
> *Life can be hard.*
> *You will be afraid.*
> *Be encouraged.*
> *Be in courage.*
> *You can do it! Really. YOU. CAN. DO. IT!*
> *Power to your elbow.*
> *Power to everything you are.*
> *Power to the person you are becoming.*
> *Power to the choices you make.*
> *Don't be tired.*
> *Be free.*

I breathe in the hope and aspiration of this playful phrase cheerfully dished out to us like rosewater and saffron ice cream. I see it stretching beyond Iran's borders, kissing the faraway horizon and marking our path forward.

These two words, *khaste nabashid*, turn anxiety into optimism, and optimism into joy.

I step forward into and through the unknown space of whatever comes next.

Fear takes its place beside me. So does courage.

Something else walks with me…many things. They glitter, waiting to be seen more fully.

REARVIEW MIRROR REFLECTION

I'm amazed at the power of affirmations, or maybe it's the power we give affirmations when we repeat them. They become touchstones that bring us back to the present moment, strengthen our resilience, and give us the "oomph" we need to go a bit further.

Khaste nabashid. Power to Your Elbow. Don't be tired. These words did wonders for me walking, and even now, Lluís and I say them to each other when a boost of courage gets us through the next wave of hurdles.

What is an affirmation, a wish, a mantra, a saying you can bring into your practice of dissolving fear and acting with courage?

WORKSHEET: WADE IN WITH WONDER

✢ Map This Myth

A Misconceived Myth

Some dreams are just too big to try.

- How has this concept, or something similar, appeared in your life?
- What version of it has held you back in a place of fear or insecurity?
- How could you dispel this myth, and in doing that, walk forward with more courage?

_____
_____
_____
_____

⇝ RECALCULATE YOUR ROUTE

Turn Here: An Affirmation to Carry With You
Life can be hard. You will be afraid. Be encouraged. Be in courage.

- What happens if this is true?
- What comes into view when you round the edge of this curve?
- How does it feel when you reach this new mile marker?

_____
_____
_____
_____

⇝ NAVIGATE YOUR WAY

Be honest with yourself. Is what you're feeling really fear? Or is it something else? How can you be more precise with what you're feeling?

_____
_____
_____
_____

What happens when you make time to see your fear, acknowledge it, and rename it with a more precise emotion? How does this reframe what you feel and the action steps you choose?

_____
_____
_____
_____

What is your normal response to fear, anxiety, and worry? What strategy or techniques help you lessen the anxiety and overwhelm associated with them as you keep greeting life?

_____
_____
_____
_____

*** *A Gentle Reminder: Be kind to yourself. You may be surprised at what comes up as you read the book. Pause to give yourself a big hug and a good shake from head to toe between prompts and chapters. Allow your nervous system to rest briefly before you leap into the next bundle of emotions.* ***

I QUIT!

EMOTIONAL WELL-BEING WARNING:

> Outbursts of anger

LOCATION: THAILAND

FEAR IMPULSES:

- *What if I fail?*
- *What if I can't do what I said I would do?*
- *How can I stay in control when everything feels too much?*
- *Will I fall short of my expectations, of other people's expectations?*
- *What if I was wrong, and this dream is impossible to achieve?*

WHAT'S IN THE IN BETWEEN SPACE?

- *Tiredness*
- *Frustration*
- *Comparison to others*
- *Overwhelm*
- *Disappointment*
- *Negative self-talk*
- *Anger*
- *Resentment*
- *Imposter syndrome*
- *Reflection*
- *Enthusiasm*
- *Love*
- *Being Seen*

COURAGEOUS RESPONSES:

- *Creating space to express frustration and anger in a healthy way*
- *Letting a breakdown happen*
- *Allowing yourself to be loved, seen, and held*
- *Surrendering the need to control everything*
- *Redirecting negative self-talk to wonder-filled contemplation*

I have an insecurity around failure, and sometimes it escalates to fear.

It started in elementary school, when rewards and recognition were tied to good grades, and, later in adulthood, when raises and promotions were awarded for excellent workplace performance.

Even without these formal institutional structures, my mind constructs its own report card, measuring many of my undertakings against a worthiness checklist, with worthiness being defined by my own high standards.

My ability–or inability–to walk two continents came under immediate pass-fail scrutiny within hours of beginning the walk in Bangkok, and it nagged at me for most of the three years I trekked westward.

I usually can identify this insecurity when my frustration, anger, and resentment boil over. Eventually, my courage, through tears and a temper tantrum, steps in to cheer me up.

❦❦❦

"Look at that guy, walking so free and easy." I cluck my tongue.

I watch how lightly and quickly he moves through the world, carrying only a small satchel, wearing sandals, unhindered in his swishing saffron orange robe. His young body is strong and agile.

He is the complete opposite of me in most physical ways.

I am strapped into a heavy backpack that tips me forward. My sun-protection strategy of long sleeves, long pants, and a runners' cap rubs me the wrong way with sweat and heat. Every step is weighted.

That guy…he's a Buddhist monk in Thailand. Me…I'm trying to be a long-distance walker who crosses two continents over a few years. Our commonalities include walking from Point A to Point B on a busy road and seeking the middle way on the noble path of life.

Today, suffering and grasping are the lessons I'm revisiting in real time.

He's not the first monk to walk past us. There have been a few others before him. Some have inspired me to put the spring back in my step. Some had me wondering about the monk's alms bowl and how to ask for what you need. This one…he breaks me.

We're only a few weeks into our multi-year walk, a couple hundred kilometers from our Bangkok starting point, and the reality of how hard this walk, this version of life, could be–will be–throws me into a bottomless pit of racing "I can't do this" thoughts.

The rising temperatures worsen towards Thailand's rainy season and creep upwards each day, 30, 31, 32, 33, and 34 degrees Celsius. Lluís and I avoid heat stroke by waking up at 4 a.m., walking during the cooler morning and evening hours, and taking long afternoon breaks in slivers of shade. But that is messing with my sleep and rest patterns. I am more tired than I thought I would be, making me cranky, negative, and fragile.

The days of delicious green curry are gone, too. My stomach can't handle it. My culinary experience in one of my favorite food places on Earth is reduced to boring fried eggs, white rice, and warm soy milk... every day.

Oh, and the freakin' dogs. We spend most of the early morning hours before sunrise fending off packs of street dogs who perceive us as strange, suspicious beings invading their turf. Lluís and I use a lot of energy tip-toeing through small towns, singing and humming The Beatles "Here Comes the Sun" and speaking sweetly to each other and these dogs, signaling with our calm voices that we are not a dangerous threat. Sometimes it works, sometimes it doesn't. Sometimes, we have to throw rocks towards them to protect ourselves from the fear they want to bite us with.

It's exhausting. It's overwhelming. It's frustrating. It's not what I expected. And I suck. I can't figure out how to make it fun, comfortable, and easier. I'm so much in my head, and one thought is on a loop: Quit!

Watching this monk walk by makes me feel like a failure, like a complete idiot pretending to be capable of achieving a ridiculous goal I dreamed up.

I am not good at failure, so I turn cynical and pummel my worthiness with self-talk.

- *Who the hell do you think you are?*
- *Walking two continents–stupid you, what were you thinking?*
- *Oh, you weren't thinking! You were fantasizing in your la-la land of go-climb-a-mountain ambition.*

- *And, Lluís, what kind of guy is he? Why would he say yes to this absurdity and walk with you?*
- *You are both foolish.*
- *None of this makes any sense.*

Frustration turns into whining.

- *I can't do this. I tried. It's too hard.*
- *I can quit.*
- *No one really believed we could do this anyway.*
- *I'm hungry. I'm tired. I'm hot. I smell gross.*
- *Everything is so irritating and aggravating.*
- *I knew it wouldn't be easy, but I never imagined it would be like this.*
- *Screw this. I'm done.*

Within seconds, whining turns into blame and resentment, spilling out in all directions.

- *Damn dogs....Thinking they own Thailand.*
- *How can people let them run around like that?*
- *We should have rested more the other day. This first month was supposed to be slower, with walking less distance and fewer hours, so we could acclimate better. But NOOOOOO, we have to get up at 4 a.m. to avoid the heat.*
- *To hell with this. Who knew January was going to be this hot? Why didn't we plan better?*
- *And that guy, that monk, walking by like he has no worries. WTF. Why can't you be like him, Jenn?*

Tsk, tsk, more tongue clucking.

I fall into a stride blinded by anger, disheartened and desperate to make it end.

In the corner of my eye, I see an irrigation ditch filled with oil-slicked water and who knows what else. I turn 90 degrees and step off the road towards the grassy, shady patch, unbuckling my chest strap. Looking down at the ditch, I yank off my backpack and hold it above my head, ready to toss it all away.

"Jenn! Jenn! JENN!" Lluís yells, coming towards me. "DON'T!"

I snap back into my body. Instead of throwing my pack in the water, I hurl it to the ground and kick it a few times with merciless fury. I collapse on top of it and let my head melt into my hands.

"I didn't expect it to be this hard every day," I say, wiping the tears from my face as I look up at Lluís.

Expectations. They give us hope, confidence, and courage to set out to try, do, and even achieve new things. They are also the false promises we create to structure our lofty plans and define success and failure. Sometimes, my expectations are too high, and I must settle for something less than the excellent grade I want. That bothers me.

Lluís extends his hand and helps me stand up again. I dust myself off, blow my nose, and shake off the temper tantrum. Lluís gives me a big bear hug, and I let him hold me for a few tender seconds before I pick up my backpack. It's nice to have someone else see you and help you through a tough moment. It's nice to be loved by him.

"Do you feel better now, Jenn?" Ah, there it is...that small but enthusiastic You can do it! voice rises back up inside me. *"Can we get back to work now?"*

"Yeah, but I don't want to fail," I mumble back, starting another inner dialoge.

Cue a long sigh.

"Um... you know you're walking two continents, right? It's not going to be rainbows and unicorns every day," the cheerleader version of me replies. *"You're tough. You'll get through it. You'll see."*

"Yeah, but I don't want to fail," I answer with a grunt.

"What does failure even mean when you're walking two continents? Ok. Forget that. Let's think about something else." The cheery voice redirects, preventing the ambitious part of me from rattling off a long list of success and failure criteria. *"You just saw a Buddhist monk. Maybe that's a sign to contemplate the right view,*

action, intention, and concentration... you know the noble path. That should entertain us until lunchtime."

Cue another long sigh.

"*Alright. Let's have it,*" I grumble, stepping back onto the road. "*Whaddya got on mindfulness as a practice for mental discipline and lowering the volume of too many loud thoughts?*"

I laugh at my own question, ready again to try, act, and walk on.

❦❦❦❦

↩ REARVIEW MIRROR REFLECTION

The irony of life, huh? We know it's rarely going to be happy-go-lucky unicorns and rainbows all the time, but how do we get so blindsided by the hard parts?

Looking back, I can see myself on that Thailand road kicking my backpack, and I want to laugh at myself for missing the cues of my lifelong tells. Frustration and anger are often my first flare-ups when I encounter self-created disappointments and beliefs about falling short of my expectations. When I think I won't get an A+ for my effort, I come undone at the prospect of getting less than a B.

I'm grateful for my fear of failure. The insecurity it triggers keeps teaching me that I don't need to be an honor student in this game called Life. I'm already passing it with flying colors...and that's enough.

What fear keeps returning in your life to teach you new lessons each time you encounter it?

⊚ WORKSHEET: WADE IN WITH WONDER

⊕ Map This Myth

A Misconceived Myth

Author William Faulkner once said, "People need trouble—a little frustration to sharpen the spirit, toughen it." Frustration toughens me, shows me where I can improve, and shows me where I am holding on too tight to my expectations.

- How has this concept, or something similar, appeared in your life?
- What version of it has held you back in a place of fear or insecurity?
- How could you dispel this myth, and in doing that, walk forward with more courage?

_____
_____
_____
_____

⇝ RECALCULATE YOUR ROUTE

Turn Here: An Affirmation to Carry With You

(Don't turn. Stay in this lane, and contemplate how the misconceived myth mentioned above may also motivate you.)

Author William Faulkner once said, "People need trouble – a little frustration to sharpen the spirit on, toughen it." Frustration toughens me, shows me where I can improve, and where I am holding on too tight to my expectations.

- What happens if this is true?

- What comes into view when you round the edge of this curve?
- How does it feel when you reach this new mile marker?

_____
_____
_____
_____

➻ NAVIGATE YOUR WAY

Reflect on these statements: Expectations fuel frustration. Expectations fuel joy.

Write about how expectations have fueled other emotions or states of being, such as anger, fear, courage, resentment, and happiness.

_____
_____
_____
_____

What flavor of anger do you most frequently identify with and notice in your life? How do you express different aspects of anger? Identify your own range of anger-related emotions or use an emotional wheel as a guide. I recommend Abby VanMuijen's version of the Emotion Wheel presented earlier in Part II.

_____
_____
_____
_____

What choices have you made when you were frustrated or angry? Where did those choices take you?

_____
_____
_____
_____

What complementary opposite emotions alleviate your frustration, anger, and resentment? What emotional trilogy harmonizes your angry flare-ups?

_____
_____
_____
_____

*** *A Gentle Reminder: Be kind to yourself. You may be surprised at what comes up as you read the book. Pause to give yourself a big hug and a good shake from head to toe between prompts and chapters. Allow your nervous system to rest briefly before you leap into the next bundle of emotions.* ***

WHY DO THEY TREAT US THIS WAY?

※

EMOTIONAL WELL-BEING WARNING:

> This story contains visualizations and an inner dialog around sexual desire, misconduct, misogyny, harassment, and profanity.

LOCATION: TURKEY

FEAR IMPULSES:

- *What is going on here? What does this guy want?*
- *This feels weird. This feels bad.*
- *Am I in real, imminent danger?*
- *Is this going to be a physical confrontation?*
- *How will I protect myself?*

WHAT'S IN THE IN BETWEEN SPACE?

- *Surprise*
- *Distrust*
- *Disgust*
- *Contempt*
- *Fright*
- *Armored up*
- *Reactive and responsive*
- *Smugness*
- *Vulnerability*
- *Shame*
- *Rage*
- *Relief*
- *Assertiveness*

COURAGEOUS RESPONSE:

- *Noticing body sensations in response to potential danger*
- *Quick-thinking personal defense actions*
- *Remembering and implementing a pre-designed safety measure*
- *Constructing a different story from outdated belief*

Growing up in a woman's body isn't always easy.

I learned early in life that men desire women. Sexual desire, where I grew up, wasn't considered a healthy expression of womanhood. Desire, I was wrongly taught, was something men had, and they may use lewd comments and inappropriate gestures to express desire.

As a teenager and young woman, I was supposed to protect myself from men's desires. Raised in a big city with big-city problems, my father, a policeman, taught me how to defend myself from unwanted leers and potential surprise physical attacks. My dad's protection strategies came like fortune cookie instructions. Walk like you're not a victim. Stay alert, don't get hurt. Carry your keys in between your fingers so you have a sharp edge if you need it. If someone grabs you, aim for the soft spots and run like hell. I walked through life thinking it was normal to carry these kinds of vigilant thoughts.

Well into my 50s, I'm still on guard with a fear of being desired too much and the fear that I won't be able to protect myself if some man's desire is overridden by his need for power and control. I still lodge a key between my fingers when I walk alone, just in case.

Awareness of these possible dangers came in handy while walking on a busy road in Turkey.

My body circulates the first alarm as I walk through a rest stop on a well-traveled road along Turkey's Black Sea coastline.

Something seedy is happening. My eyes take in what my tense fists, shoulders, and jaw have already calculated. A few trucks and cars idle on the far edge. A woman with a short dress and bright, fire-engine red lipstick leans into a car window. I feel the men's eyes scan my body, and it's not just because I'm carrying a backpack, an unusual site in those parts. It's my blonde ponytail, which I know they see.

"There," a man in a brown car says with just enough English, jutting his chin forward. He's referring to Lluís, who walks ahead of me further up the road.

"*Evet*. Yes. I know," I nod with a half smile and a smatter of Turkish. I attempt to be polite and discreet. Right now, with the hairs on the back of my neck standing on end, I prefer to be unseen or, better, invisible. But as I've discovered, prudence is my backup plan... the same prudence I've learned growing up as a woman in a man's world.

As if sensing someone is thinking about him, Lluís turns back sooner than expected and, with one arm, waves in a big sweeping gesture. I wave back.

Lluís and I walk at different speeds. It's exhausting for me to keep up with him, and it's hard for him to slow down to stay with me. Over thousands of kilometers, we developed our own sign language to communicate two basic things: A one-armed wave is "I'm okay, keep walking," and two arms crossed like an X is "Stop and wait." We send signals back and forth all day long, roughly in 10-minute increments.

Beyond the rest stop, I hug the shoulder's guard rail. Walking in the same direction as traffic makes me nervous because I can't see what's coming from behind me. Soon, we had to go through a tunnel, which terrified me more, and walking with traffic was our safest option this time.

Concentrating on walking faster than I'm used to so I can get through the dreaded tunnel sooner, I'm blindsided by the man in the brown car. He drives behind me, slowing down and making other cars pass him. Through the open passenger window, he makes lewd movements with his tongue, and his right hand grabs his crotch. I look at him with disgust.

The man, leering, amused with himself, steers closer, beginning to shift diagonally into my walking space. I feel my face and body shift from surprise to "Don't fuck with me" contempt.

My mind keeps running the risk assessment. A thought pops in: What about the whistle? I wear a whistle around my neck for walking emergencies, but I'm downwind from Lluís, and with the traffic noise, the sound won't reach anyone.

My hands move quicker than my brain. They start pulling off the day pack I carry on the front of my body. I undo the buckles of the chest and the hip straps of the heavier pack fastened to my back, getting ready to leap out of that and run if I have to.

In fractions of milliseconds, my mind has imagined and plotted out a half-dozen worst-case scenarios, including one scene that pings with a red flag of an immediate threat: If this man blocks the road's shoulder, traps me between his car and the guard rail, jumps out of his car, and physically accosts me, what am I going to do?

My brain assesses whether he manages to get that far and whether any number of other threats might follow.

Again, the man tries to lure me into his car, leaning over to unlock the door and saying things in Turkish that I don't understand.

My heart races. I tremble. Imagining what people could do—what this one person could do to me—pushes my fear response into "Get out of here" flight mode.

From somewhere inside me, I hear, *"Act crazy."* So I do.

Putting on my best tough girl from New Jersey attitude, I go apeshit crazy. Letting my body take over, I know I may have a chance to protect myself if I can pretend to be more insane than this man can handle. I become a lunatic woman on a rampage.

I throw down my day pack and lodge a key I keep in my pocket between my index and middle fingers in case this offensive and repulsive man gets too close, and I have to jab a soft spot of his flesh. Like the whistle, the key is another act-quick security technique my father taught me when I was 13. "You just need enough time to run," my dad said as he instructed the aim of the sharp part of the key toward an imaginary attacker's eyes, throat, inner thigh, or the soft spot between the thumb and index finger.

Fear begins to turn to rage. I growl and howl at the top of my lungs like a banshee set on fire.

Then I see it all. The man who grabbed my ass when I was 20. The teens who tried to fondle my 32-year-old breasts in a crowded square. That other disgusting guy a few months ago who unzipped his pants in the car as I walked by. Etc. Etc. Etc.

"Why do men think they can treat women this way?" I roar. There was no way this guy in the brown car in front of me now would get away with that.

I stand up straighter. I lean forward. I look into the eyes of this creep.

"You want a piece of me," I scream. "You better call the hospital right now. Because if you get any closer to me, or if you get out of the car, that's where you're fuckin' goin'. The hospital, asshole."

Somewhere in this chaotic moment of rage, something more than courage rises up. Bold moves of self-preservation rear their head. I move into "defend my space" fight mode.

I raise my right fist, key tip exposed. My left-hand lifts to block my face, adopting a stance I learned long ago in a handful of karate and kickboxing classes.

"Come on," I smirk and flick my fingers toward the man, daring him to think again about who he's messing with. "I'm going to make you regret that you even looked at me."

I feel my mouth twist to show my fangs. I transform from being scared and vulnerable to a vengeful warrior woman determined to right every wrong committed against any woman throughout human history. My fright turns into revenge.

I glare at the man, convinced I'm going to battle…convinced I'll win if we do.

He flinches. I see it. He cowers behind the car's steering wheel and becomes the small man he is. A glimmer of smugness sweeps through my body. I want to believe I shocked him with the same amount of fear he sparked in me.

I guess I did because it worked. The man hit the gas and sped off in the same measure of milliseconds that ignited my distrust, disgust, contempt, fear, and courage. He vanished into fast-moving traffic before I could write down his license plate.

Lluís, unaware of the raving mad scene I created, turns back at the scheduled interval. I cross my arms in an X to signal, "Stop. Wait." He sends the same signal back and leans on the guard rail.

I'm infuriated. My body wobbles with nervous energy. I mutter strings of expletives and evil-eye curses in the direction of the man in the brown car. Lluís sees my agitation before I reach him.

"Are you okay?"

"No." My hands quiver as I recount the story.

Lluís kisses my forehead and holds my hand. He shakes his head, repulsed by men like this who call themselves men.

I steady myself. We start walking again with our flashlights on and head into a tunnel. In this part of Turkey, there are few alternative walking paths, and the tunnels are the most viable option for getting from Point A to Point B. Tunnels scare me on a normal walking day. This one, right now, casts an even darker shadow.

Still shaking, it takes all my mental strength to stay focused on the next step and right behind Lluís on the small sidewalk lining the tunnel wall.

Concentration doesn't stop my mind from wandering. It doesn't stop my body from feeling vulnerable. The tears come, and so does shame.

While I know the shame is on the man in the brown car, a question pokes at my inner seams, *"Did you provoke him?"*

"No. I just walked by," some other part of me responds.

"Do you think that your reaction was warranted?" Something judgemental inside me jeers.

Disjointed memories flood in. Flashes of how I covered my body as a teenager, as a young woman, as a midlife professional, as a long-distance walker in my 40s, so often choosing modesty–or was it invisibility?–over desirability. Glimmers of my dad teaching me self-defense moves to keep the boys at bay. Glimpses of debates I had with colleagues about the rape culture we grew up in and how it's normalized. Flickers of lifelong doubts halted my confidence in situations I assessed I couldn't control.

"Was this my fault?" surfaces from nowhere. I don't even recognize that as my voice.

"Hell, NO! Jenn, stop this… RIGHT NOW. That guy is a scumbag. He will have his reckoning for the shit he's done. You are a tough, brave woman who can stand up for herself. Keep walking. Hold your head up high. Get out of this tunnel. It's okay. You're okay," a guardian angel whispers to me.

I wipe away my tears. I take a deep breath. I walk a little faster. The light at the end of the tunnel pulls me out of my bubble and back into the world.

Yes. I'm okay.

🍀🍀🍀

↩ REARVIEW MIRROR REFLECTION

I will never know what the man in the brown car intended. I have no idea if he planned to hurt me or if he was amusing himself at my expense. And, honestly, from where I'm sitting now, I don't care whether I overreacted or not.

What I know for sure is that the actions I opted to take matched my gut feeling, and I won't ever apologize for that. Something was off; something felt weird. My body was in a state of fear-induced distress. I trusted my instincts to respond. In that moment, life in the form of a sleazy man tested my grit, and my grit won.

I'm more aware now of the conditioning I either learned or taught myself about being on guard when showing my beauty to men.

So many times in my life, I have consciously and subconsciously turned up or down my shine depending on the probability of receiving catcalls and crude stares.

It's so demeaning and demoralizing. As a young adult, I hated feeling that I had to armor up before going out dancing with friends, and even now, it bothers me that I occasionally look over my shoulder to make sure no one is following me. Will we ever live in a world where that's not necessary?

Sitting at my kitchen table writing this, I wonder: How can I shine brighter with all of my inner and outer beauty in situations where I may feel inclined to hold myself back and trust that I know how to keep myself safe?

Have you ever wondered about that, too? Have you figured out how to do that?

⊙ WORKSHEET: WADE IN WITH WONDER

⊕ Map This Myth

A Misconceived Myth

Women have to armor up in superhuman ways to protect themselves.

- How has this concept, or something similar, appeared in your life?
- What version of it has held you back in a place of fear or insecurity?
- How could you dispel this myth, and in doing that, walk forward with more courage?

_____
_____
_____
_____

⇝ RECALCULATE YOUR ROUTE

Turn Here: An Affirmation to Carry With You

I love my body. I love everything it knows. I love how it expresses itself. I trust my body.

- What happens if this is true?
- What comes into view when you round the edge of this curve?
- How does it feel when you reach this new mile marker?

_____
_____
_____
_____

⇞ NAVIGATE YOUR WAY

When did disgust, contempt, or similar emotions appear in your life? How did you respond to it?

_____
_____
_____

What infuriates you or fires up your rage? What is underneath your fury?

_____
_____
_____
_____

How is shame connected to other emotional, mental, or physical states, internally generated or externally provoked?

_____
_____
_____
_____

How do you recognize the rage or shame distress signals in your body? How do you move your body's red-flag signals out of your fear zone and into action steps that keep you safe?

_____
_____
_____
_____

*** *A Gentle Reminder: Be kind to yourself. You may be surprised at what comes up as you read the book. Pause to give yourself a big hug and a good shake from head to toe between prompts and chapters. Allow your nervous system to rest briefly before you leap into the next bundle of emotions.* ***

THE HEAVINESS OF GRIEF

EMOTIONAL WELL-BEING WARNING:

> This chapter discusses death and talking to and receiving messages from loved ones who have passed.

LOCATION: THAILAND (AND SEVERAL OTHER COUNTRIES)

FEAR IMPULSES:

- *How will I measure up?*
- *Am I not doing enough?*
- *Am I failing in this new role?*
- *How can I still miss you so much?*
- *Am I doing right by them?*
- *Will they appreciate what I'm doing for them?*
- *Are they disappointed in me?*

WHAT'S IN THE IN BETWEEN SPACE?

- *Loss*
- *Grief*
- *Nostalgia*
- *Responsibility*
- *Guilt*
- *Regret*
- *Remorse*
- *Contemplation*
- *Justification*
- *Admiration*
- *Comfort*
- *Love*
- *Tenderness*

COURAGEOUS RESPONSES:

- *Harmonizing the sad bits of grief with joyful memories or actions*
- *Opening space for divine and/or higher-self guidance and wisdom*
- *Staying in the question and not bypassing emotions when they feel mushy*
- *Breaking a repeating pattern of doubt and discouragement*
- *Surrendering the doubt and walking on*

Grief and regret mingle in unsavory ways, especially when I am alone and lost in my thoughts, thinking about the choices I made and evaluating if they were good ones. These two emotions show up when I overanalyze "would have, could have, should have" situations that I can't go back and change, but I can't let go of either.

Sometimes, these feelings come when I'm wound up in my head

with my lifelong insecurity around failure–and whether I am doing enough not to fail. More commonly, though, I feel grief and regret about something I couldn't do for someone else when they needed my help or a sense of loss for something that has changed that I couldn't stop from changing. While grief also comes from feeling the loss of a loved one, the regret part is often linked to my people-pleasing tendencies, another lifelong disposition I'm unraveling and mending.

I saw grief and regret tug at my heartstrings while walking in Uzbekistan, Iran, Turkey, Italy, and France, but I will share with you here something that happened to me in Thailand.

❦❦❦❦

"Thanks, Mom!" I squat down to the ground, perfecting my newly acquired skill of balancing my body and backpack while not tipping over headfirst. A shiny *baht* coin goes into my pocket. The Thai baht is worth pennies, about 2.5 cents in U.S. currency, but each coin I find makes me feel rich, like a million bucks.

∼

The coins carry magic with them, I told Lluís a couple of weeks earlier.

Soon after we left Bangkok, Lluís started finding roadside coins almost every day. He found so many so often that I started to get jealous.

And then, in the hardest, hottest moments of the day, I started to find coins too. They appeared when I complained about being hungry and tired and when I most missed my old, non-walking life.

Noticing a new pattern emerging, I saw how the coins turned my gripes into gratitude and my insecurities into sanctuary. "See a penny, pick it up. All that day, you'll have good luck," I cheerfully recited the rhyme I learned as a kid each time a coin twinkled in my direction.

One day, Lluís found seven coins! That was a record amount for a long time on our walk, all the way through Asia up until Iran. "I guess your grandmother loves you a lot," I joked, watching him claim another prize. The more coins we found, the more I began to see them as gifts, tokens of love, from our angel ancestors.

"I think they are signs showing us that we are being watched over... that we are protected... that we're on the right path..., and that we should keep going," I said, trying to convince him about our walk's divine and spirit-guided aspect.

Believing in coin-discovery serendipity on a multi-year foot adventure across two continents feels meaningful, perhaps even mythic. Adding to the folklore, I have assigned the coins he finds as otherworldly hugs from his beloved late grandmother and those I find as encouraging embraces from my dear deceased mom.

Lluís rolled his eyes. He's not into woo and mystic mysteries. He thinks the coins fell out of the pockets of the two, three, and four family members huddled together on mopeds zipping by us at any given time. Yeah, I guess that's an option, too.

～

Like most of the coins coming my way, today's coin, my first baht of the day, shows up right when I need it. I've tangled myself up with too much brooding about foolish things that shouldn't matter.

Long-distance walking gives me too much time to think...and overthink.

On my best days, in the most boring moments, my walking reflections lead to complex problem-solving formulas for the Earth's worst ills. In the longest, emptiest stretches with nothing else to do, I pretend to end world hunger, climate change, gender inequality, war, greed, and the misuse of power.

More often, though, the complex problems I'm trying to fix are those inside my own head. I start connecting the dots of what once was, what is now, and what could be. Sometimes, I marvel at all the effort that got me to this right-now, present moment, and I admire the gorgeous, multi-dimensional map of my life I made for myself. I also frequently mull over past mistakes and regretful choices, and feel guilty for not doing more or better.

Glancing at the rows of sugar canes lining both sides of the road, I fixate on something I can't change, something that happened years before that, even if I wanted to change, I couldn't. I can't remember the string of thoughts that pushed me into this rabbit hole, but suddenly, I am in an avalanche of remorse and apologies to my sister.

"Mom, do you think I wronged her?" Since we walk at different paces and Lluís is too far ahead of me to talk to, I've started talking to my mom. I talk to her more these days than I did when she was alive... another sorrow scratching my heart.

"She asked me for help. She asked me to go there, and I didn't go. I couldn't fly back when she needed me. I had a lot of work then."

I watch a farmer carry a pile of sugar cane to an empty part of the field. I let the space between thoughts widen and appreciate the quiet time when I lower the volume of my mind's constant chatter. I wait for some sign, a cosmic nudge of knowing, but I'm in no rush for a spiritual reckoning.

"You know, Mom, I was a little bit mad about it. How oddly timed some of it was."

I lean against the guard rail, yielding to the fully loaded truck racing to the sugar processing plant.

"But still...maybe I should have gone back? Isn't that what sisters do?"

I am waiting for an answer, but not sure I want the one that may come.

"I don't know, Mom. I don't know my role as a big sister anymore. Now that you're gone and we're all adults with our own lives and choices, I don't know how to keep my promise to you. I don't know how to look out for my siblings without rushing in like Saint Jenn to save the day. What's most helpful? Most needed? What's too mothering? Too smothering? What's the right balance?"

The questions recast themselves into contemplative meditations.

"Who am I to my siblings?"

A long pause. I wait. Nothing.

"Who do I want to be to them?"

Another long pause. I wait. Nothing.

Then come the justifications.

"*I want to be kind, generous, compassionate, and dependable... with boundaries. That's fair, right?*"

"*I don't want to be the righteous one, the fixer, the rescuer...*"

"*Not that she asked me to be or do any of those things. She asked for a hand, and at that moment I couldn't....wouldn't... help her.... Mom, see what I mean? I'm so confused. Things feel so complicated. What should I do, Mom?*"

My heart drifts to sadder places.

Glimpses of memories roll in.

Mom in the hospital, thin but still smiling. Me leaning down to listen to her fading heartbeat. Playing "Go Fish" with her during chemotherapy. Mom on the couch in our Barcelona apartment. Mom and Aunt Carol giggling while sipping wine in California. Mom gardening in the backyard, trimming her purple-blue rhododendron shrub. Mom decorating my childhood home with way too many Christmas lights. Mom dipping a piece of bread into the pot tasting the sauce. Mom folding laundry. The first snow…flurries for her funeral.

"*Mom, I miss you. I wish you were here…not here as on this road in Thailand…but here, close by, a phone call away. I miss your voice. I miss your laugh. I miss your meatballs and gravy. They were so delicious!*"

I cry…for my mom, for me, for the time we had, and for the time we lost.

My heart stirs, and after a while of being alone with life, the sad heaviness of grief slowly drifts out of me.

Comfort comes as a whisper. That's how I hear wisdom.

"You're being hard on yourself. It happened years ago. You made a decision. It was not a big deal…no one was hurt; it didn't damage your relationship," I hear from the inside out. "You both love each other and are closer now than before. Let it go, Jenn. It's nothing… it's not something to lose your head and heart over."

I take a long inhale and tune into the frequency of the message.

"*Yeah. Why am I losing my head over this? How did I fall again into this pit?"* I pull out my mp3 player and hit play on my feel-good 80s playlist. *"Time for a reset."*

Just as the first notes of Journey's "Don't Stop Believing" float into my single earbud, I step over a baht coin. I step backwards and bend over far enough to confirm that it's a coin and not a piece of metal trash.

"Oh! Thanks, Mom!" I squat down and claim my second win of the day. Holding the coin in my hand, I feel the warmth of a loving and familiar embrace.

"I love you, Mom. I miss you. Yes, I will walk on. I know you still walk with me, too." I dust off the coin, kiss it to the sky, and put it in my pocket. Some coins I use along the way, some coins I save. This one is mine forever.

Lluís waits for me up the road.

"You okay?" He squints, trying to make out why I've been crying.

"I'm okay." I reach for his hand. "I was just talking to Mom about some stuff that happened. I feel better now."

REARVIEW MIRROR REFLECTION

Losing a parent is heartbreaking, and a piece of you dies with them. The hurt of losing my mother to cancer in 2008 still pokes a hole in my heart now and again. Instead of pushing the feeling away, I surrender to it and let tenderness lead for a little while.

In her absence, I wrangled with myself for many years about what role I wanted to have in my extended family. I was afraid of both being too much and not doing enough, uncertain of how to care for their needs while taking care of myself. I went through different periods of being the peacekeeper, the mediator, the one who rushed in, the doer, the fixer, the counselor, and then, throwing up my arms with exasperation, I was the one who didn't want to get involved anymore.

Now, I've found my way to being a sister-friend, the one who listens, the one who cares but doesn't leap headfirst to tidy everyone else's mess, and the one to laugh with. I'm a work in progress. I think my mom would be proud of me. I feel she is.

How do you hold regret and grief? How do you turn the fear of being left behind into a flavor of courage that rings with harmony and love?

I'm sending you a lucky coin and a hug from afar as your heart steers you through these big thoughts.

WORKSHEET: WADE IN WITH WONDER

✢ Map This Myth

A Misconceived Myth

Grief is better hidden away. Nothing good comes when I let myself or others see my sadness. If I just toughen up enough, the sorrow will pass.

- How has this concept, or something similar, appeared in your life?
- What version of it has held you back in a place of fear or insecurity?
- How could you dispel this myth, and in doing that, walk forward with more courage?

_____
_____
_____
_____

⇢ RECALCULATE YOUR ROUTE

Turn Here: An Affirmation to Carry With You

Grief needs time and is worth my time to express. I can learn how to greet and embrace regret and grief. Acknowledging them when they are present in my mind, body, and heart makes them less difficult to hold.

- What happens if this is true?
- What comes into view when you round the edge of this curve?
- How does it feel when you reach this new mile marker?

_____
_____
_____
_____

↠ NAVIGATE YOUR WAY

When has regret clouded your choices? What fear hid behind those clouds?

_____
_____
_____
_____

What sadness or loss needs more space and time for mourning? Have you grieved enough, or have you masked your grieving?

_____
_____
_____
_____

What is one thing you cannot change but still hooks your mind into a spiral of thoughts? What do you believe is the lesson you're meant to learn when that happens?

_____
_____
_____
_____

How can you recast regret and grief into inquisitiveness, acceptance, and gratefulness? What kind of coin, love token, or symbol helps you move forward with a bit more courage?

_____
_____
_____
_____

*** A Gentle Reminder: Be kind to yourself. You may be surprised at what comes up as you read the book. Pause to give yourself a big hug and a good shake from head to toe between prompts and chapters. Allow your nervous system to rest briefly before you leap into the next bundle of emotions. **

WHEN YOU CAN'T FLEE, NEGOTIATE

EMOTIONAL WELL-BEING WARNING:

> This chapter contains tense and aggressive situations and encounters with multi-generational hate, xenophobia (fear of strangers) and fear of change.

LOCATION: BOSNIA AND HERZEGOVINA

FEAR IMPULSES:

- *Oh, f*@#! We're in danger!*
- *How will we get out of here?*
- *Are they going to hurt us?*
- *How are we going to protect ourselves?*

WHAT'S IN THE IN BETWEEN SPACE?

- *Anguish*
- *Hate*
- *Grief*
- *Melancholy*
- *Unsettled jitters*
- *Humiliation*
- *Aggression*
- *Tension*
- *Imminent danger*
- *Fright*
- *Helplessness*
- *Vulnerability*
- *Hopelessness*

COURAGEOUS RESPONSES:

- *Choosing to de-escalate tense and aggressive situations instead of adding fuel to the fire*
- *Using previously learned techniques and practices to mediate through conflict*
- *Staying calm even when it's hard to do so*
- *Knowing when it's better to back down, fight, or flee*
- *Watching how other people respond in tense moments and learning from them*

There is so much suspicion, mistrust, and hate in the world. We see it every day in the news. Some of us experience it firsthand daily, wherever we live. Some of us carry these attributes with us through our ancestral lines; distant and indistinct feelings passed down through generations of surviving war, poverty, societal upheavals, and sweeping changes don't always usher in the best qualities of humanity.

I am the granddaughter and daughter of people who lived through World War I, the Great Depression, World War II, and the Vietnam War. My grandparents, in their lifetimes, were born in one country and died in another. They lived through the border-shifting and life-changing political tags of monarchy, communism, and democracy. That's just a surface-level view into the heavy cross-cultural baggage my family shoulders.

While my grandparents were able to rise above their situations and create better opportunities for their children and grandchildren, I still feel the weight of the struggle–their struggle to live healthy and prosperous lives in periods of great change and uncertainty, their struggle to protect what they earned, and their struggle to let go of misgivings about what other people could take away from them.

Walking through the Balkans, the region of my paternal lineage, many of these fears landed right before us. They tested us in profoundly uncomfortable and heartbreaking ways. Here's how they surprised us one particular night and how we de-escalated an unexpected, aggressive situation.

❦❦❦❦

A car door slams below in the parking lot.
Thump. Thump. Thump. Thump.
People are running up the stairs.
Thump. Thump. Thump. Thump.
That's my heart in my throat.
It's dark. People running upstairs towards us is a bad thing...a really bad thing.
I nudge Lluís. He's awake, too.
Only the mosquito net part of our tent protects us. We were sleeping–we thought safely with permission from local townspeople and a police officer–in the attic of a small stone building, now used occasionally by a visiting doctor and nurse, in a speck of a village in the Croatian Catholic section of Bosnia and Herzegovina.
Earlier in the evening, we noticed several plastic crates filled with

empty beer bottles, a tattered couch, and graffiti scribbled with a marker in the far corner of the room. People, probably young people, from the village come here often. We hoped they wouldn't come by tonight.

Our luck runs out at 10:30 p.m.

∼

This Balkan country is still so clearly dealing with the horrors of centuries of war while trying to overcome its past and boost itself up the world's economic ladder.

Tourists who trickle in will find Bosnia and Herzegovina's medieval villages, the capital city, religious pilgrimage sites, mountains, and national parks charming and beautiful.

Refugees, migrants, and forcibly displaced people no European country wants to harbor see none of this beauty. They walk at night with the hope of staying invisible and with the dreaded fear of stepping on a landmine left behind from the 1990s war that tore Yugoslavia apart and slowly returned sovereignty to its six republics. One night, I hear these refugee footsteps passing on a small road near our hidden campsite and send loving-kindness thoughts in their direction and further down the road: *May you be safe and protected. May you be healthy and strong. May you find food and shelter. May you be free, happy, and live with ease.*

Lluís and I, the walkers, well, we see everything else. We see the red signs with a white skull and crossbones nailed to trees warning of explosives in the area. And the bullet holes and shrapnel lodged in abandoned houses. And the hate graffiti and initials of radical political parties spray painted on walls and street signs. We see the sadness in the eyes of a cautious people with a long memory of strife and division living in a transitional economy without the promise of a fruitful future. Ghosts haunt empty villages where families fled and never returned.

Growing up in the United States did not prepare my heart to hold what it was witnessing here. Neither did my many years of global travel, during which I saw everything from the poorest of the poor to the richest of the rich. Two years of touching the Earth with my feet did not make me ready for this place either.

Bosnia and Herzegovina became an unexpected place of ancestral clearing, made stranger because my paternal family roots are planted across the border in nearby Croatia. What's a line on a human-invented map when soul work and family-energy healing seem to be important guiding factors?

When we were planning the walk, I knew parts of the Balkans might be difficult for me. Growing up, I heard lots of stories about "us" vs. "them." At university, I studied some of the region's geographical and political history. I have visited other parts of the region several times before. I have a vague understanding of how people are divided by religion and unified by culture and language.

And still, I am completely caught off guard emotionally and psychologically.

Most days, for a month of walking in this country, I weep. I sob with an unfamiliar hurt I can't pinpoint. I cannot shake off the despair clinging to me. While the country is in a fragile state of recovery, the anguish, the grief, and the melancholy I carry come from somewhere else. They are emotions I haven't ever felt this strongly anywhere else. Something cellular was handed down to me from long-ago and never-known Balkan ancestors. I feel it in my bones. It makes my blood run.

To alleviate some of the heaviness, I consciously and deliberately try to plant forgiveness and love with each footstep. I imagine those wishes rolling off my shoes like new seeds dropping into this old piece of land. I till the soil with hope. But even wishes can feel onerous.

～

Earlier this afternoon, we stopped at a bar for a cold soda. I chit-chatted with the bartender with my basic-intermediate Croatian, but his friendliness ended after I paid the tab. He had a look about him…a look that hinted at "Two strangers walk into a bar they don't belong in…" It's not a joke or laughter I saw in his face. It was wariness.

While sipping my orange Fanta, Lluís and I started plotting our end-of-the-day routine. Given the landmine situation, we couldn't risk wild camping off the road, and we're not in touristic places with hotels. There's a church up ahead; we'll go there. Churches, mosques, temples, and cemeteries have been safe havens for us for several years of walking.

Before reaching the church, we waved to an elderly woman working in her garden with her teenage grandson and granddaughter. Considering the country's political climate and the numerous passport checks we faced throughout the Balkan region (an attempt to deter refugees and asylum seekers from crossing into the European Union), we instinctively opted to introduce ourselves to the neighbors. We thought it would be safer for all of us to let them know we planned to camp near the church.

Jumping between Croatian and English, the grandson suggested that we stay in a small stone building across the way from their garden. "The attic is open. You could sleep there," he shrugged as if it were no big deal.

Taking that as permission, we hauled our packs up the narrow flight of stairs and set up our sleeping spot.

As we pulled out our mosquito net, another neighbor rushed up the attic and gruffly asked why we were there. We told him our story, and he rushed off, mumbling about us being foreigners.

We guessed he was the one who called the police because, a short time later, we were again explaining our story as the policeman took pictures of our passports. Not overly concerned about our presence, he gave us a bag of freshly picked plums from his garden and left us with an off-hand comment, "I'll tell the neighbors you are Christians. It won't be a problem," an assumption he makes because our passports are from countries where Christianity is the main religion, an assumption he makes because he thinks the neighbors will yield if they believe we are part of the "Us" circle and not the "Them" group.

At sundown, about 8 p.m., we tucked ourselves into our sleeping bags, grateful to be safe indoors.

Thump. Thump. Thump. Thump.

I nudge Lluís. He's awake, too.

Startled, we stay in the tent for a few seconds, silently deciding what to do.

Four men form a semicircle around our makeshift campsite and block our only exit. Shining flashlights in our faces, they demand that we slowly get out of the tent's mosquito net.

"What are you doing here? How did you get this address?" one of them asks in broken English. I smell alcohol on his breath.

We don't have time to be afraid yet, but we instinctively know these men could attack us physically if they don't trust us. Everything about their being, body language, and tone of voice is aggressive.

I start a rapid-fire, what-are-we-going-to-do evaluation in my head.

Should we push through the men and make a run for it?

No... we're barefoot, we won't get far, they'll chase us. Things will get worse if we run.

Can we fight them?

No... we're outnumbered; they have brute force and are bigger than us. Lluís will do his best to protect me and vice versa, but it won't be enough. I rule out that option but spread my legs wider, at a slight diagonal, and position my hands and body into the fight-ready mode, subconsciously preparing to defend myself if they come closer.

Standing there scared, not finding enough Croatian words fast enough (it is not my native language, and I am not fluent in it), I freeze. But no one notices. All eyes are on Lluís. He's the one they want.

I follow their gaze. I know Lluís is also calculating the risk and measuring the next right action. I see it on his face.

A natural mediator, Lluís diplomatically defaults to the technique we learned in Thailand: Speak softly when a pack of dogs barks loudly.

In a calm, almost congenial voice, Lluís slowly and clearly explains to the wolves in human form who we are, where we live, where we are walking from, where we are going, and why we are sleeping there.

With the mastery of a Jedi, he uses the cadence of his voice to describe the nice elderly woman across the way and her grandson. (Ironically, they turn out to be the mother and son of one of the men in front of us.)

The tension lessens among the four men as Lluís proves we're not a threat. They move their flashlights off our faces and shift their footing.

I sense my own righteousness, and I have to temper right now. I have an immediate impression that if we were darker-skinned people, suspected to be from non-Christian countries, suspected not to be a European-American couple, we would be kicked down the stairs and maybe beaten.

I'm disgusted at the thought that I share a common ethnicity with these bullies. We are in the Croatian Catholic part of Bosnia and Herzegovina. My lineage parallels theirs, and their deep-seated, xenophobic mistrust rouses me to stand on higher moral ground. I have to keep this bottled up and stay unaccusing to keep us safe.

Lluís holds up the bag of plums. "See. A policeman came, took pictures of our passports, and gave us these delicious plums. Would you like one?"

I look at Lluís with pride. I am constantly amazed to learn new things about how he intuitively navigates situations and how his intuitive reaction is sometimes so different from mine.

The middle-aged man whose mother and son steered us here rumbles with discontent.

"We have to control who comes to our town. We don't want terrorists here," he says. He has the air of being a king without a throne but lacks the wisdom to realize how unimportant his little spot of a village is in the bigger scheme of life to anyone but him.

"The police have no authority to say you can sleep here. If he was so concerned, he should have taken you to his home for the night," another man retorts. I refrain from asking what authority he has in this decision and instead let Lluís lead.

Lluís won't engage in slinging blame and keeps sweet-talking about our day, what we saw, and how we got a soda at the bar. He's stalling. He's building trust. He's slowing down the anger and suspicion. He doesn't know which direction this confrontation will go. No one does. It's very unsettling.

I do my best to lean towards a rational line of thinking. They are not going to hurt us. That would cause an international problem. They are trying to do what they think is right–protect their families, homes, and community. My dad would do the same. Lluís would do the same. Not in this way, never in this way, but I could see could each of the men I love most taking a protective stance if they felt their loved ones were threatened. The problem is discerning what is a real threat.

I wish the old woman would come and speak sense to these men. She knew we weren't a danger. She'll dissuade these men from using violence. She's the matriarch. I tilt my head towards the stairs, hoping to hear the old woman's footsteps. They never come.

A few minutes pass, an eternity. Lluís is still talking. The men's tempers fizzle. The aggression tapers off. Boredom, drunkenness, or lucidity finally convinces the men that we are "the good ones." They give us their permission to sleep in the attic and file down the stairs and back into their cars.

We don't sleep well. We don't think anyone else will return, but we're fidgety the rest of the night. I'm angry, too, pissed off about the state of the world and the hate that's becoming normalized in so many places. I'm bitter that, in the places we've been, people who have similar bloodlines to mine, behave with such hostility towards "The Others." I drift off, unsure we're safe, but too tired to think more about it.

The next morning, sitting on a bench eating an energy bar before we set out, I watch dawn change the sky. I take a long inhale. Everything is better at daybreak.

Until it isn't.

"Did you sleep well?" The middle-aged man from last night appears behind us.

Ignoring the man's semi-conciliatory tone, Lluís shows his fangs with a glare that could make the dead turn over in their graves. In daylight, awake, and without the other bullies around, Lluís makes it clear forgiveness is not an option.

The man looks down to the ground, littered with plastic bottles and empty cigarette packs.

"Is this yours? Did you do this?" the man grills, again ready to pick a fight.

"No! These are YOUR PEOPLE who do this. We carry our trash out," Lluís snaps.

Fawning. That's my reaction now. My body slumps forward as I process the men's words, tone of voice, and body language.

I hold my breath, thinking, *"This can't escalate again. They'll find us down the road if it does. Please just appease him, and let's go."*

I see in my mind's eye how quickly things can unravel. I put on my backpack and touch Lluís' arm. "C'mon, Love. It's not worth it."

It takes a long time to find our walking rhythm. We're unsteady.

We talk about what happened, the threat to our safety and their safety, our responses, and what we learned from it.

Soon, we fall quiet. Silence stabilizes us.

More than any other country, Bosnia and Herzegovina seems determined to teach me something new every day.

I want to see it, but there is nowhere safe for me to look.

※※※※

↩ REARVIEW MIRROR REFLECTION

You never really know when a potentially dangerous situation could fall on you. You don't know when a circumstance will challenge everything you thought you knew about yourself. You don't know who will show up to teach or guide you and how that lesson will be given to you. And you may not recognize the moment when you get wind of the fact that you are the one who has been called to help clear some hard-to-describe hurt that has been passed down through generations.

Those things, wrapped in between unexpected heart-opening

kindnesses and unforeseen troubles, happened to me in Bosnia and Herzegovina. Nothing in my life had prepared me for what this country, this small corner of Europe, showed me, yet everything in my life had prepared me for it, too.

No, I hadn't ever before walked so close to the tragedies of war. But, in Bosnia and Herzegovina, my capacity to empathize with people who suffered that fate expanded.

No, I hadn't ever before faced xenophobic hate so close to my face. But, in Bosnia and Herzegovina, my compassion for people who regularly experience that brutality swelled.

No, I hadn't ever faced a situation where everything in me told me to run, and I could not flee. But in Bosnia and Herzegovina, I learned how to negotiate through fear, and that taught me something new about my courage.

No, I hadn't ever before felt so deeply linked to my ancestors and the lives they may have lived centuries and generations ago in a place similar to the land my feet touched. But, in Bosnia and Herzegovina, my connection to a past I didn't know has begun to shape a more informed path for my future.

Whether we know it or not, life always creates opportunities to test us, break our hearts, and show us how to walk on with toughness and tenderness.

I am strong, sensitive, and steadfast. Thank you, Bosnia and Herzegovina, for reminding me of that.

Can you recall a moment in your life when you encountered an ancestral hurt that needed acknowledgement or healing before you could continue on your spiral path?

☉WORKSHEET: WADE IN WITH WONDER

⊕ Map This Myth

A Misconceived Myth

Our collective, global history does not affect us. What's done is done.

- How has this concept, or something similar, appeared in your life?
- What version of it has held you back in a place of fear or insecurity?
- How could you dispel this myth, and in doing that, walk forward with more courage?

_____
_____
_____
_____

⇝ RECALCULATE YOUR ROUTE

Turn Here: An Affirmation to Carry With You

Despite your history, you can resolve to find strength, courage, and dignity to recover, rebuild, and recommit to making a better life for yourself, your family, and your community.

- What happens if this is true?
- What comes into view when you round the edge of this curve?
- How does it feel when you reach this new mile marker?

_____
_____
_____
_____

⇴ NAVIGATE YOUR WAY

When have you felt a fight, flight, freeze, or fawn response to fear? How did it feel in your body?

_____
_____
_____
_____

What part of your lineage holds the scars of war, genocide, poverty, or other atrocities? What can you learn from the past to help you move through fear today?

_____
_____
_____
_____

What previously learned life lesson helped you move through a possible life-threatening fear?

_____
_____
_____
_____

How have you been courageous in the face of physical danger?

_____
_____
_____
_____

*** *A Gentle Reminder: Be kind to yourself. You may be surprised at what comes up as you read the book. Pause to give yourself a big hug and a good shake from head to toe between prompts and chapters. Allow your nervous system to rest briefly before you leap into the next bundle of emotions.* **

BREAKING AWAY FROM EXPECTATIONS

※

EMOTIONAL WELL-BEING WARNING:

> In this chapter, there are mentions of the hardships of couplehood, separation, and loneliness.

LOCATION: TURKEY

FEAR IMPULSES:

- *Should I go at it alone?*
- *What if I can't do it by myself?*
- *What would I miss out on if I chose this route instead of the other one?*
- *Will he be okay without me?*
- *Who is right, and which idea is more valid?*

WHAT'S IN THE IN BETWEEN SPACE?

- *Disappointment*
- *Discontent*
- *Stubbornness*
- *Inadequacy*
- *Wondering*
- *Self-Assurance*
- *Boldness*
- *Fortitude*
- *Independence*
- *Determination*
- *Restfulness*
- *Innocence*

COURAGEOUS RESPONSES:

- *Evaluating many options and choosing the one that feels most heart and spirit aligned*
- *Being with and moving through discomfort*
- *Taking time off to rest, play, and simplify*
- *Testing what happens when you go at it alone*
- *Asking for help*
- *Accepting help when you don't think you need it, but really do*

In my practice of cultivating *courage mindfulness* (let's dub it that), I'm learning that, like fear, courage has its own disguises, alternative expressions, and nuances that may be valuable to pinpoint as we collectively expand our emotional literacy.

My courage may be loud or quiet, forceful or reserved, depending on the moment. It may be interpreted as confidence, foolishness (I prefer foolhardiness), or virtuous. It may be a heroic life force that helps me claim greater independence and freedom. Courage may cause loneliness, separation and isolation when I break away from other people's expectations just as much as it may build my fortitude, endurance, and resilience.

However you come to courage, or however courage comes to you, it's important to see it as something that may start a cycle as much as it finishes one. Courage may guide you through fear, help you close a chapter of life, and lead you to something amazing. Courage may also bring you to an unknown edge where unfamiliar fears await– fears that will test you in inconceivable ways because you're meant to learn new lessons.

Courage multiplies courage. The more awareness you have of being courageous, the more courage you can draw up and the braver you'll feel.

Likewise, too much courage, too much of the time, may weaken your nervous system if it's left unchecked and unregulated. If you stay on high alert in an anxious, fearful state for extended amounts of time, you'll flood yourself with adrenaline and cortisol. That kind of forced, always-on courage could be draining on your body and damaging to your organs.

So, what is the path of courage? I questioned this when Lluís and I separated for a few weeks in Turkey, and I met other hikers who gave me a new perspective on courage.

❦❦❦

This is a Russian fable told to me by Elena, a hiker I met in Turkey.

A gaggle of geese are preparing to fly south for the winter. A crow wants to join them and travel to this faraway place.

"It's a long, long way," says one of the geese. "Are you sure you want to come?"

"It's okay. I am power crow," the crow replies, proud of himself.

The geese set off and, many hours later, found a place to rest for the night. They wait for the crow.

An hour or two later, the crow finally arrives, huffing and puffing.

"Crow, are you okay?" a goose asks.

"Yes, yes. I am power crow," he says, shaking off his tiredness.

The next day, the geese get ready to leave again. The crow says he wants to continue with them.

"Crow, are you sure? It's a long, long way," says the goose, concerned about the crow's ability to fly onwards.

"Yes, yes. I am power crow. I will go with you," the crow says, convinced he can make the journey.

Off they go, flying for hours and hours. The geese settle down late in the day and wait for the crow. One, two, three hours pass. No crow. Finally, late in the evening, he arrives, exhausted.

"Crow, are you okay," says the worried goose.

"Yes, yes. I am power crow," the crow says, tired but enthusiastic.

The next morning, the crow, again, says he will join the geese.

"Crow, it's a long, long way," the goose says again, unable to deter the crow.

"I am power crow," the crow says stubbornly.

They fly and fly and fly. And, the geese, again, finish their day, waiting for and wondering what happened to the crow.

Hours pass. One, two, three, four, five hours. No crow.

Suddenly, the geese hear a big crash. SMACK! The crow slams into the ground, so fatigued he can barely stand up.

"Crow, my goodness, are you okay?!?," exclaims the goose.

"Yes, yes. I am power crow," says the crow, winded and finding it hard to catch his breath. "But, you know what? I am also idiot crow."

My new friend Elena and I laugh.

I look away from the always-burning fires of Chimaera, the mythical land of the fire-breathing lion-goat-serpent monster of Greek legends. It dawns on me, and I say, "I am idiot crow."

Elena chuckles. After trekking together for a few days, she knows the truth in my statement. I have been struggling to keep up with the group of Russian hikers who have taken me under their wings. I had to choose to take an easier, alternate route because I wasn't confident enough in my ability to walk up and down mountainous trails with my heavy backpack. But still, she believed in me.

"No. No. You are power crow," she says, throwing her fists up and shaking them victoriously.

"Yes, yes. I am power crow," I say, joining her in the celebratory pose. "But, you know what? I am also idiot crow."

We both smile.

Sometimes, we are power crow. Sometimes we are idiot crow. Sometimes, too, we are both power crow and idiot crow at the same time. Still, we fly on.

∼

I'm sitting with Elena and her hiking companions in southern Turkey, near the Mediterranean Sea because I'm not with Lluís; Lluís is following a route he invented along the Black Sea in northern Turkey.

A few weeks ago, the burden of walking and being together 24x7 for many months at a time and force-fitting our individual dreams into a compromise neither of us was fully happy with had reached a boiling point.

Over winter break, when the weather was too harsh to walk safely, and we lulled ourselves back into a normal life with the comfort of good food, a warm bed, and easy living, Lluís and I went head-to-head about the route we would follow when we restarted the walk in the spring.

For Lluís, the walk IS the adventure. The other things we happen upon fuel his desire, but they are secondary events. Walking from Bangkok to Barcelona is the most significant goal. He believes starting at Point A and finishing at Point B is the big, black-and-white picture aim. His personal anthem is "Never give up," which means tackling things persistently, methodically, and consistently until they are done.

Lluís, with his male way of doing things, wants to stick to the plan, walk a set distance most days, and continue walking the route in Turkey he mapped out years ago when all this was still a dream.

I understand him. I, too, am ambitious, determined, and

headstrong when I have a goal to achieve. I like structure. I like getting gold stars for effort. I like feeling successful at different milestones.

But I also have a woman's heart. On this trip, my heart wants to speak louder than my logic, intellect, or drive. Actually, my heart wants to win and is willing to fight for the win.

I want to change our route and explore long-distance, coastal hiking trails I learned about in southern Turkey, routes used by the ancient Lycian and Carian peoples. I want to step through time and walk the land that connects different ethnic groups, languages, customs, and trade around the Mediterranean. We traced the north coast of the country in the fall; in the spring, I wanted to experience another region.

Years back, when we were planning the walk, I knew Turkey was going to be one of my highlights. I wanted to go through this place at a much slower pace, stopping frequently to appreciate its culture, food, and history. I didn't want to rush this part of the walk. I wanted a relaxed pace. I wanted to play. I wanted to see what we would see without hurrying to be somewhere else.

I laid my cards on the table with Lluís.

I told him what he knew and what we had discussed many times before. For me, the walk is a vehicle through which we can experience the world in ways we never imagined. The walk is like a tour bus, making many stops along the way and, eventually, steering us home to Barcelona. Aligned with my style of wanderlust, we can hop on and off the "walking bus" when our eyes, hearts, and spirits find a pretty rest stop, and then we can hop back on any time we feel like it and go any direction we want westward, homeward.

Lluís wants to finish a task. I don't want the walk to be a task. He wants a direct and prescribed route that shortens the distance of a long journey between two destinations. I need more flexibility and freedom in how, when, and where we walk; for me, the destination is whatever we find along the way.

Our argument descended into a shouting match, each of us becoming more obstinate in defending and justifying our positions.

Exasperated, I call it quits: I don't want to walk with him for six weeks.

"The walk has won. It has consumed us. It has chained us to itself. This walk has broken me, us, and I'm sick of it." I cry and scream at the same time. "I need to step away from the walk so I can love it again. You insist that your way is the only way. But it's not. You invented this way; we re-invent it everyday walking, and I don't want to go that way anymore."

We fell apart emotionally. Sadness, stubbornness, and fighting to be right blocked our vision.

"What are you saying? Are we over? Or are we separating for a little while?" Lluís sniffled, teary-eyed. We have fought more in two years of walking than in the ten years we lived together. This walk has tested us in every way and keeps showing us how differently we think, walk, and function.

"I'm not saying I want to break up. I'm saying I don't want to walk the path you're insisting we walk. I see another way, and I want to try it. You are welcome to come with me. If you don't want to, we'll meet up later and try walking together again." I said that out loud to him, but in my frustration, I really didn't know if what was broken could be fixed.

∼

Sitting at a beachside cafe in Antalya sipping strong Turkish coffee, the comforting and familiar deep blue color of the Mediterranean Sea and the sun glittering on the waves pull my eyes away from the maps I'm marking up for future reference.

The mountains hugging southern Turkey's shoreline make me nervous. They are bigger than I expected and ringed with clouds of uncertainty.

I don't know exactly how I will get over them alone. If I can do it, that will be a first for me. I worry that my backpack is too heavy to manage these ascents and descents; the extra weight shifts my center of gravity, and I get scared when I'm off-balance.

I don't know how I will make it westwards to Çanakkale, where I will meet Lluís six weeks from now.

I don't know yet about any of the experiences waiting for me in and beyond the mountains. The many people, like Elena and her hiking friends, who would show up to help me when I needed it (and when I didn't think I needed help) are still strangers. The mini panic attack I will have when I get lost and have to recalculate my route without a GPS signal is about a week away, not even on my radar screen. The time off I will take from walking to relax, volunteering at an orange grove, and painting trail markers for other hikers are not even concepts yet. Or the yoga festival I will stumble into, where I will serendipitously remember to breathe again, and where I will feel weightless and free.

It's all a mystery to me what comes next on my still-being-invented route. And it's all mine for the making.

Looking at the horizon, I don't know if I will be a power or an idiot crow. All I know is that I need to fly.

REARVIEW MIRROR REFLECTION

The choice to break the expectation that I was only meant to walk with Lluís on a route we had planned to do together shocked even me when it happened. I didn't want that to be the choice, but I knew I needed that space in our relationship and from the pressures of life inside the walk.

Equally dumbfounding was that, up until the last minute, I expected Lluís to change his mind, give up his plan, and walk with me in southern Turkey. For a while, I was angry that he didn't change his life to fit my desires.

Ultimately, in this situation, I'm glad he didn't come with me, and I'm glad I didn't bend to please him. There are times and places where negotiation and compromise work wonders. This was not one of those times, and having the discernment and courage to cut the cord of expectation proved necessary and valuable.

Even though it wasn't always easy to do this piece mostly by myself, and even though I didn't walk as much of those trails as I thought I would, the experiences I co-created with Spirit and my inner intuitive guidance led me to some of the most enriching opportunities of the entire walk.

I strengthened my capacity to be independent, learned how to ask for assistance when needed, and accepted help when I wasn't aware that I needed it. I opened my heart to be with whatever and whoever showed up without worrying about a specific daily outcome. I allowed myself to stop when pushing myself for no good reason felt unnecessary. I gave myself time to choose other soulful options that aligned better with the messages I received from my body and heart instead of letting my mind's prodding thoughts force-feed decisions.

There's more than one way to go into your heart of courage. Being willing to leave behind some of your own and other people's expectations is one starting point.

What expectations have you cut away so you could feel free, independent, or whole?

WORKSHEET: WADE IN WITH WONDER

Map This Myth
A Misconceived Myth
Courage is always heroic and intrepid.

- How has this concept, or something similar, appeared in your life?
- What version of it has held you back in a place of fear or insecurity?
- How could you dispel this myth, and in doing that, walk forward with more courage?

_____
_____
_____
_____

⇥ RECALCULATE YOUR ROUTE

Turn Here: An Affirmation to Carry With You

Courage can be quiet or loud. It can be worn with a cape of confidence or foolhardiness. It can bolster resilience and fortitude. It can wear you down or help you break free from expectations that hold you back. Courage can be whatever you want it to be. You can choose how it comes to you and how you receive it.

- What happens if this is true?
- What comes into view when you round the edge of this curve?
- How does it feel when you reach this new mile marker?

_____
_____
_____
_____

⇻ NAVIGATE YOUR WAY

What expectations were you afraid to break? Where did you fear falling short?

_____
_____
_____
_____

Where have you masked your fear with an exaggerated need to be right and prove "them" wrong? Did this pave a bold way forward or bubble-wrap you in bravado?

_____
_____
_____
_____

When did you have to be a power crow? When was courage the thing you needed most to get you where you wanted to go? When have you been an idiot crow or, said more politely, when did you take an ill-advised path that proved to be an unwise choice? When did you have to be strong and foolhardy, so that you could fly higher and soar longer?

_____
_____
_____
_____

Imagine looking out over the horizon, calculating your path up and over the mountains you see before you. How do you map the way forward emotionally, mentally, and spiritually? What will you pack with you to help you navigate the trail?

_____

_____

_____

_____

*** A Gentle Reminder: Be kind to yourself. You may be surprised at what comes up as you read the book. Pause to give yourself a big hug and a good shake from head to toe between prompts and chapters. Allow your nervous system to rest briefly before you leap into the next bundle of emotions. ***

THE WOW! FACTORS

EMOTIONAL WELL-BEING WARNING:

> This chapter mentions historical choices influenced by war and political changes.

LOCATION: THE FRENCH-CATALAN BORDER

FEAR IMPULSES:

- *We're so close to success. What could mess it up now?*
- *Why is this still so hard?*
- *Are my choices adding up to something purposeful or meaningful? And meaningful to whom?*
- *Is my effort worthwhile?*

WHAT'S IN THE IN BETWEEN SPACE?

- *Pride*
- *Satisfaction*

- *Significance*
- *Melancholy*
- *Respect*
- *Connection*
- *Inspiration*
- *Alignment*
- *Anticipation*
- *Wonder*
- *Awe*
- *Thankfulness*

COURAGEOUS RESPONSES:

- *Pausing to remember how many times you had to pick yourself up to get where you are now*
- *Savoring the effort it took to accomplish a goal and the choices that helped you succeed*
- *Acknowledging where your success may have been built on the shoulders of other people's efforts, failures, successes, and choices*
- *Allowing wonder and awe to fuel your choices*

The sweetness of achieving a goal quiets fear, at least for a little while.

Give yourself a moment to remember something you achieved and still treasure.

Can you remember the tremendous physical and mental energy it took to reach that goal? And the pit-in-your-stomach fears and insecurities that initially held you back? And the courage you chose to embody so you could succeed?

Now, rewind the memory reel a little further back.

Can you begin to see how your parents, grandparents, and generations of your family encountered all sorts of hardships and how the choices they made, with or without trepidation, helped, over time, to lift you higher?

If you rested in this pause, would you be able to cherish the uncountable numbers of choices–yours and other people's–that led you to this present moment?

Lluís and I had a morning to do just that when we reached the French-Catalan border, so close to home. It filled us with wonder, awe, and gratitude.

🐞🐞🐞🐞

"I have a surprise for us!" Lluís exclaims, rummaging through his backpack. "Ta-da!"

He pulls out a chocolate bar and unwraps it with the enthusiasm and affection it deserves.

"I've been saving it for this moment. Welcome to Catalonia, my love! WE DID IT! We're home, and Barcelona is right there," he points southward down the Mediterranean shoreline. "You first. Take a piece."

Lluís carried this prize for months through Italy and France, and this place, Coll de Belitres, the border between France and Catalonia/Spain, marks the final stretch, the last ten percent, of our walk.

With ninety percent completed, we take stock of where we've been...and who we've been.

"Here's to us!" I break off a big chunk, ignoring the sugar crystals forming on the edges. I raise it as a toast to our fortitude, particularly to the endurance I needed to muster to make it through these last few weeks.

Like us, this chocolate bar has survived the changing spring weather–rain, frigid cold, melting snow, mud, blustery wind, and debilitating heat–and everything else thrown in our direction.

We also had heavy-footed animals snooping around our tent. They were probably boars, but we didn't dare leave our shelter to find out. Sometimes, in certain situations, I think it's better not to face what scares me directly. Sometimes, I want to pretend that my fear doesn't exist and that I can hide from it.

Oh, and the pain and discomfort of doing hard things! You would think it would get easier to walk uphill and downhill carrying a heavy load, to blaze a new trail on abandoned pathways, and to keep on carrying on. But it doesn't. Just when I think I'm winning at this game called Life, niggles of apprehension and nervousness show up in other dramatic ways.

Fortunately, for now, those hard bits are behind us. Inching closer to Barcelona, our final destination coming into view, we celebrate the journey with the simple pleasure of chocolate and a heartfelt tribute to the effort it took us to get this far.

Lluís has a speech ready, caring words about the wonder of it all, of how we started out in Thailand so long ago with this ginormous, lofty dream of walking home, and the astonishing accomplishment of arriving at the Catalan border, years later, together.

We walk down memory lane, recalling some of the highs and lows that have left an indelible mark on us individually and as a couple…the people, places, challenges, extraordinary kindnesses, and experiences that make us smile. We are teary-eyed and satisfied.

We sit on a stone overlook looking straight into the sea with strong gusts of wind hurting our ears, proud and in awe of our achievement. We stare with reverence for Mother Nature's gorgeous grace right in front of us.

"Wow! It's amazing. We're amazing." I gaze at the Catalan coast, already knowing where the winding road will take us. We are in familiar territory. We have hiked here before, and we know how the curves bend. Still, it's all new again to us. It's a different moment, a different time. We are not the same people we were before the walk. Or are we?

As we honor how far we've come and take comfort in knowing how close we are to completing a significant personal goal, other feelings bubble up.

Melancholy is one of them. The memorial signs erected at this now-defunct European border crossing tug at those heartstrings. Hundreds of thousands of people desperately passed this exact spot in the late 1930s, hoping to escape the Spanish Civil War and political turmoil that would become the Franco dictatorship. Lluís' great-grandfather, grandparents, infant father, aunts, and other relatives were among them.

In early 1939, with winter still blowing a bitter north wind, Lluís' family–his grandmother carrying her one-year son, Lluis' dad, in her arms–stood in a long queue with thousands of others waiting to step into the greatest unknown they would ever experience. They left everything behind and fled as refugees, determined to survive. It would take them years to return home.

His family's decision to leave and the choices that had to be made in the face of terrifying fear shaped Lluis' father's life, which shaped Lluis' life, which now influences and shapes my life.

I see similar patterns in my own family. My Croatian grandparents left their homeland when communism made life too hard for them, and their choice to start over again in the United States changed the course of my family's story forever. And my choice to live in Europe affects my family and Lluis' family.

I take another bite of chocolate. New feelings surface to replace the sadness that was just there. Respect, honor, and a connected sense of belonging swoop in. Then comes the wisdom: My success links to the many multi-generational choices my grandparents, parents, and other ancestors made decades and centuries before me.

My mind connects the dots. It refers to a blog post I wrote in 2016 for our Bangkok Barcelona On Foot website, one of the first posts documenting our walk. It was called "We Are All Connected."

At one of the many police stops between Tak and Mae Sot, the last Thai town before crossing over to Myanmar/Burma, we ate sugar cookies offered by one of the policemen. At the same time, groups of young Burmese huddled together, waiting to get their passports and IDs checked. The ones without identification or those with false documents were pointed to the back of a pick-up truck.

A few miles up the road, two pick-ups passed us. As they drove by,

I tumbled into a flood of thoughts that later became these written reflections.

> "My existence is the result of several generations of coincidences. I am the daughter, granddaughter, and great-granddaughter of immigrants. I am one direct outcome of the choices, risks, challenges, and opportunities taken by people who came before me, and I carry this ancestral connection as a gift and a source of strength to try to live my best life…
>
> Rules, nationalities, passports, borders, ways to keep people out, ways to keep people in. We can't single-handedly change the system. There is too much to change and right now, that is not our purpose. All we can do now is share and connect our light and love. We can hope that all our collective light clears a safe and compassionate path for everyone on this roadside."

Sitting at the French-Catalan border, ruminating over what was and what will be, I imagine a wide ripple of overlapping circles and spirals of lives gone by and lives being lived now. The center of each spiral is labeled "Live your joy," and the message spreads over countless layers.

There is much to consider when reflecting on how so many paths converge and diverge, where fear and courage move with the same breath but lead to so many different outcomes.

Hardship, insecurity, disappointment, anger, shame, grief, perseverance, resilience, equanimity, trust, joy, wonder, awe, failure, success, anticipation, willingness and so many other felt but unnoticed emotions have their place in the space between the fear that stops us and the courage we need to step forward.

At the intersection of my heart, mind, body, and soul, I hear the whisper:

What will you choose?
How will you choose?
And in the choosing, who do you become next?

"Wow! Just WOW!" I smile taking it all in. Lluís reaches for my hand. We look off into the distance, our eyes following the meandering road stretching beyond what we can see.

"Ready?" I ask, grabbing the strap of my pack.

"Yes!" Lluís scrunches the chocolate wrap and puts it in his pocket. We leave no trace that we were here, but we both know our light and love connect us to whatever came before us and will connect us to whatever is yet to come. "Let's go home."

I nod, pick up my walking sticks, and walk on.

※※※※

REARVIEW MIRROR REFLECTION

Success comes with a bundle of emotions.

Contentment, satisfaction, and pride certainly may show themselves as congratulatory phrases ringing with, "You did it! You reached a goal. WOW! You did that thing you said you would! WooHoo! What a fantastic and well-earned accomplishment!"

If you scratch that surface and look deeper, other feelings may also exist. There could be sadness as one phase of life–an ambitious phase–comes to a close. Or there may be wonder and curiosity as the omnipresent "What's next?" question surfaces. Maybe there's awe for showing up for yourself and your dream. There could even be a beautiful feeling of completeness, wholeness, and oneness to all there is, to all there was, and to everything that could be.

What do you feel when you are at the cusp of achieving something significant and meaningful?

⊚WORKSHEET: WADE IN WITH WONDER

⊕ Map This Myth

A Misconceived Myth

We are all on our own individual journeys, and each of our journeys is independent of everyone else's. My path is unique, and the burden of walking it is mine alone.

- How has this concept, or something similar, appeared in your life?
- What version of it has held you back in a place of fear or insecurity?
- How could you dispel this myth, and in doing that, walk forward with more courage?

_____
_____
_____
_____

⇉ RECALCULATE YOUR ROUTE

Turn Here: An Affirmation to Carry With You

> *I am an island unto myself. I am self-reliant, aware, compassionate, and emotionally and intellectually mature. I take refuge in myself and my willingness to keep greeting life.*
>
> *I am also part of the collective–living, gone, and yet to come–and part of a family lineage that also stepped through choice points that led to outcomes that, over time, led to my here and now.*

Both concepts have created ripples that influence the shape of my life.

- What happens if this is true?
- What comes into view when you round the edge of this curve?
- How does it feel when you reach this new mile marker?

_____
_____
_____
_____

≫ NAVIGATE YOUR WAY

What do you see when you sit on the top of your mountain of success and achievement? What fears tried to stop you from reaching the peak? What helped you turn that fear into courage?

_____
_____
_____
_____

What dots can you connect in your own life when you look back and see, wonder about, or imagine the choice points your parents, grandparents, and ancestors encountered? What outcomes rippled far and wide beyond their individual decisions?

_____
_____
_____
_____

What does awe feel like to you, and what does it inspire?

_____
_____
_____
_____

What is one thing you're willing to do now to live your life on purpose, with joy, and aligned to an intuitive higher calling?

_____
_____
_____
_____

*** A Gentle Reminder: Be kind to yourself. You may be surprised at what comes up as you read the book. Pause to give yourself a big hug and a good shake from head to toe between prompts and chapters. Allow your nervous system to rest briefly before you leap into the next bundle of emotions. ***

DROP THE SHIELD YOU HIDE BEHIND

Writing a book is a great teacher of fear and courage. Sitting down to put words around these ideas and lessons I have carried for years showed me new things about myself and my patterns.

During the developmental edit of this book, I kept intuitively getting the message, "Stay with each chapter, with each emotion. Feel it. Know it. Breathe with it. Then move forward with it from that emotional center."

No matter how fast I wanted to go through the editing process, I felt like I was in a pond slipping on mud, chest-high in murky water. It was a very uncomfortable place to be stuck in, and so different from the lightning speed that usually moves me into action.

Wading into the pond of my mind, I was afraid to feel all these feelings again, to feel them out loud through words on digital paper, and to linger in their energy.

Staying in these muddy waters for a few weeks brought unexpected clarity on two things.

1. WHAT I CALL FEAR MAY BE AN INSECURITY THAT CHIPS AWAY AT MY CONFIDENCE.

Unraveling insecurity frees my mind from old beliefs that no longer serve me and helps me to dispel myths about myself that are no longer true, if they ever were.

My confidence flows easier when my tangled-up emotions around fear and insecurities are exposed and embraced, and I give them space to say what they want to say to me. Insecurities and negative self-talk based on false fears dissolve when I pause to listen to my thoughts, feel my emotions, and intentionally practice self-compassion.

2. COURAGE HAS BEEN MY SHIELD AND MY SWORD. MAYBE I DON'T NEED THEM IN THIS WAY ANYMORE.

I grew up in a time when the way to win and succeed was to push the fear aside and march on with fearless ambition. One day, before I started rewriting portions of the book, I received an image while meditating. I saw myself lifting a giant shield and walking through life with my shield always up and the sword in my other hand slashing a path forward.

This visualization made me realize how I have used courage, not from a heart-centered place but frequently from a mind-centered place. My mind constructed a shield to protect myself from feeling too much fear and insecurity. The solution for many of my problems was simple—put on my big-girl panties, trudge forward, and ignore whatever else I felt.

Now, I wonder every morning as a new day dawns: How can I drop my mind's shield, sword, and the brute force way of being brave? How can I let my heart guide the cultivation and practice of a new version of courage I would like to embody at this phase of life?

While nearing the book's final edits, I told my dad about these revelations. He offered another image that stays with me now. "If you're in a pond and slipping in the mud, imagine all the trees around you. Reach for the vines and branches dipping into the water. Use them to guide your way through and pull yourself up out of the muck. Keep doing that until you reach a safe spot on the shore."

And with that, we come full circle to where we started, but another rung higher on life's spiral path.

We can wade into and move with the fear that comes to us.

We can slip and slide on the emotional mud.

We can guide ourselves forward with the courage we find, invent, and discover in the murky waters.

We have what it takes to survive and thrive with fear, courage, and everything in between.

Each time we do this, we strengthen the muscles of our fortitude and resilience.

We learn which invitations from life are genuine and which ones to welcome with a big, wonder-filled YES!

Our choice points become easier to see, and the decisions we make become bolder, more aligned with our true desires. Our choices become more soulful, purposeful, and joyful.

It's okay to be with our fear. It's okay to be with all the other emotions. It's okay to have different versions of courage we experiment and expand with as we grow, learn, and live the life that keeps calling us forward. And it's okay to release fear and courage when they are less needed, and see what else guides our hearts.

Choose your adventure from fear to courage. Begin again in the liminal space. Make the in between a journey worth remembering.

Slowly, slowly, you will go far.

༄༄༄༄

Oh…and take your map and compass with you. It may come in handy!

132   THE IN BETWEEN

For your onward journey, which emotional stepping stones will you choose to guide you into your heart of courage?

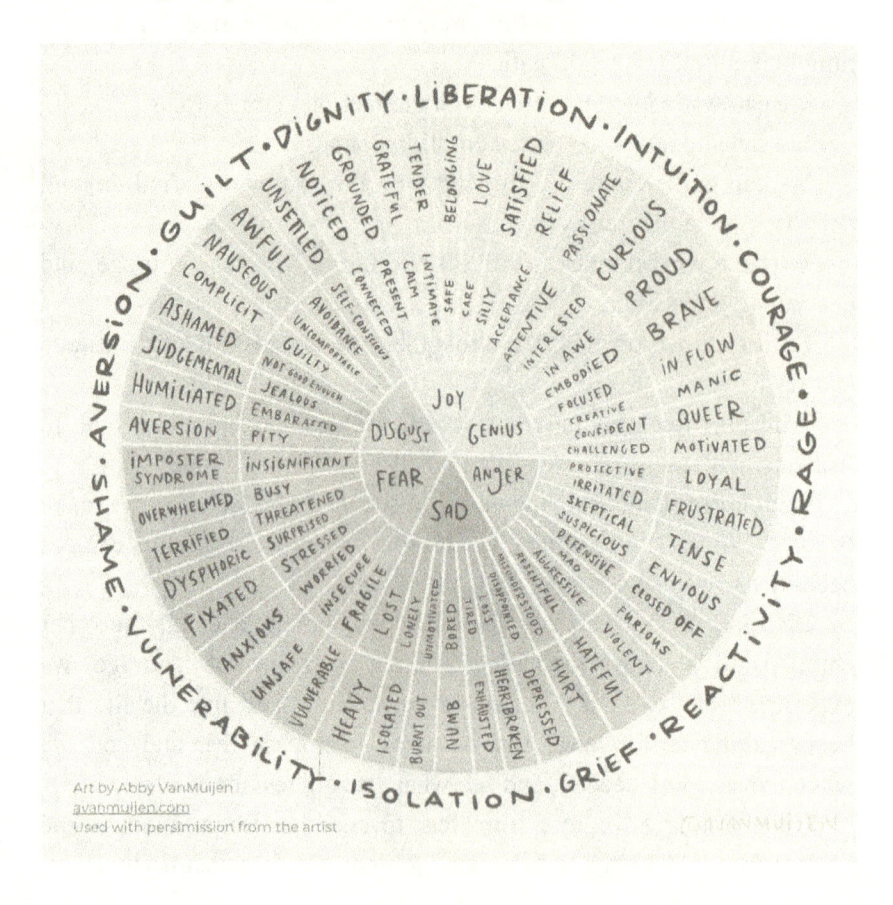

Art by Abby VanMuijen
avanmuijen.com
Used with persimission from the artist

How will you navigate your way forward? Keep iterating your map and use *The In Between* compass to course-correct as you go.

Designed by Jenn Baljko

AFTERWORD

BE BRAVE. BE BOLD. BE FREE.

"De nit, vull ser lliure, no valenta."
"At night, I want to be free, not brave."

I see this message written in Catalan every time I leave my house, and I nod in agreement when I pass the brick wall it's spray painted on.

The message scribbled in red is a call to stop violence against women and allow women of all ages to walk freely and safely at night without fear. It appears on walls and elaborate murals all around Catalonia.

Whenever I see these five words, something hits home for me. I feel stronger and walk taller. I, too, don't want to walk with fear.

More than anything, the truest thing I have ever wanted is freedom–full freedom in every way that it is possible to be free. I want to be free to live the way I want, and I don't always want to be brave to make this wish possible. I just want to be. Do you want that, too?

Being brave–being in courage–feels most useful to me when it sparks my inner joy and, with a brighter expression of inner joy, expands my sense of being unencumbered, limitless, and sovereign.

It occurs to me now, as I write these final pages, that in order to achieve the kind of freedom I deeply desire, I have to keep working at understanding what holds me back. It's a constant job to unravel the cocoon I weave for myself. It reminds me of something else I read on a wall years ago.

> *"Qui no es mou, no sent les cadenes."*
> "Those that don't move don't feel [notice] the chains."

Lluís and I stumbled on this quote (attributed to Rosa Luxemburg, a key figure of the revolutionary socialist movements in Poland and Germany during the late 19th and early 20th centuries) in September 2015, a few months before we started our Bangkok Barcelona On Foot walk. Walking in a Barcelona park, the bright purple bougainvilleas caught our eyes before we saw this string of graffiti. Then, we saw these words…and could never forget them.

Years later, I remember this adage in much the same way I remember *khaste nabashid,* power to your elbow.

These phrases weave together as meditative mantra.

> *Move and notice what chains me.*
> *What stops me from living the life I want?*
> *See, name, and face the fear that holds me back.*
> *Shift my mindset.*
> *Learn my emotional language.*
> *Practice greeting life.*
> *Be less tired and more willing.*
> *Choose to live in the heart of courage.*
> *Be brave.*
> *Be free.*
> *I AM FREE.*
> *Fear breaks the shackle.*
> *Courage charts the path.*
> *In between, I live it all.*

I send you off, dear reader, with this wish.

May you continue to find your way through your fear and insecurities. May you live to know your heart of courage. May you play and prosper in the space in between.

Power to your elbow, brave one!

THANK YOU

Thank you for accompanying me through this book. I am so glad our paths intersected.

In many ways, we are in the liminal space of one ending point and another starting point.

As we finish the book, I hope the chapters, worksheets, and journaling prompts have offered you a new perspective. Take time to rest with and integrate what you have learned. This is a beautiful place to be!

If you want to explore beyond these pages, here are a few ways we can continue the journey together:

- Visit alwaysonmyway.com to learn about my Mindful Writing Mentoring program and upcoming events.
- Access a free mini-masterclass about fear and courage here, alwaysonmyway.com/the-in-between-book.
- Join my Facebook group, facebook.com/groups/fierceawakenedwoman.
- Start a book-related conversation in your community (See the reading guide in the next chapter).

- Invite us to speak at your event. Bring the Bangkok Barcelona On Foot documentary to your organization. Lluís and I are available for virtual and in-person events (depending on the location and timing). Contact us via jenniferbaljko.com/documentary.

With a hand on my heart, I wish you the best. May the wind whisper sweet things to you, and may you move toward your dreams with grace, gratitude, joy, and wonder.

Follow us on Instagram:
@jennbaljko
@bangkokbarcelonaonfoot

READING GUIDE

In addition to the worksheet prompts at the end of each chapter, I offer these questions as another way for you to create a meaningful and sincere conversation.

- How do you define fear?
- How do you define courage?
- What are you afraid of?
- How long have you held this fear?
- How has this fear, or others, shown up in your thoughts and emotions? Describe what happens when you feel fear-full and where you feel it in your body.
- How does fear get your attention? What signals does it send your mind and body?
- What other emotions surface when you think about or feel fear?
- Which emotions help you confront, manage, dissolve, and/or transcend fear?
- How do you discern fear from insecurity, anxiety, worry, or other emotions that rattle you?

- How do you know when you have shifted from being in a state of fear to being in a state of courage?
- What does courage feel like to you?
- How has your courage evolved throughout childhood and young adulthood to now?
- What other emotions feel close to courage, and how can you better use these other emotions to make bolder decisions?
- How could you choose to live in the heart of your courage? And what becomes possible if you do that?
- What happens when you arrive at a choice point in a state of fear? In a state of courage?
- How is courage always with you?
- How is courage something you can continue to cultivate and practice?

BANGKOK~B...

ESLOVÈNIA
CROÀCIA
BÒSNIA-HERCE...
TURQUIA
GEÒRGIA
AZ...

CATALONIA   FRANÇA   GRÈCIA
BARCELONA   ITÀLIA

ÀSIA A PEU 🐾 ON FOOT

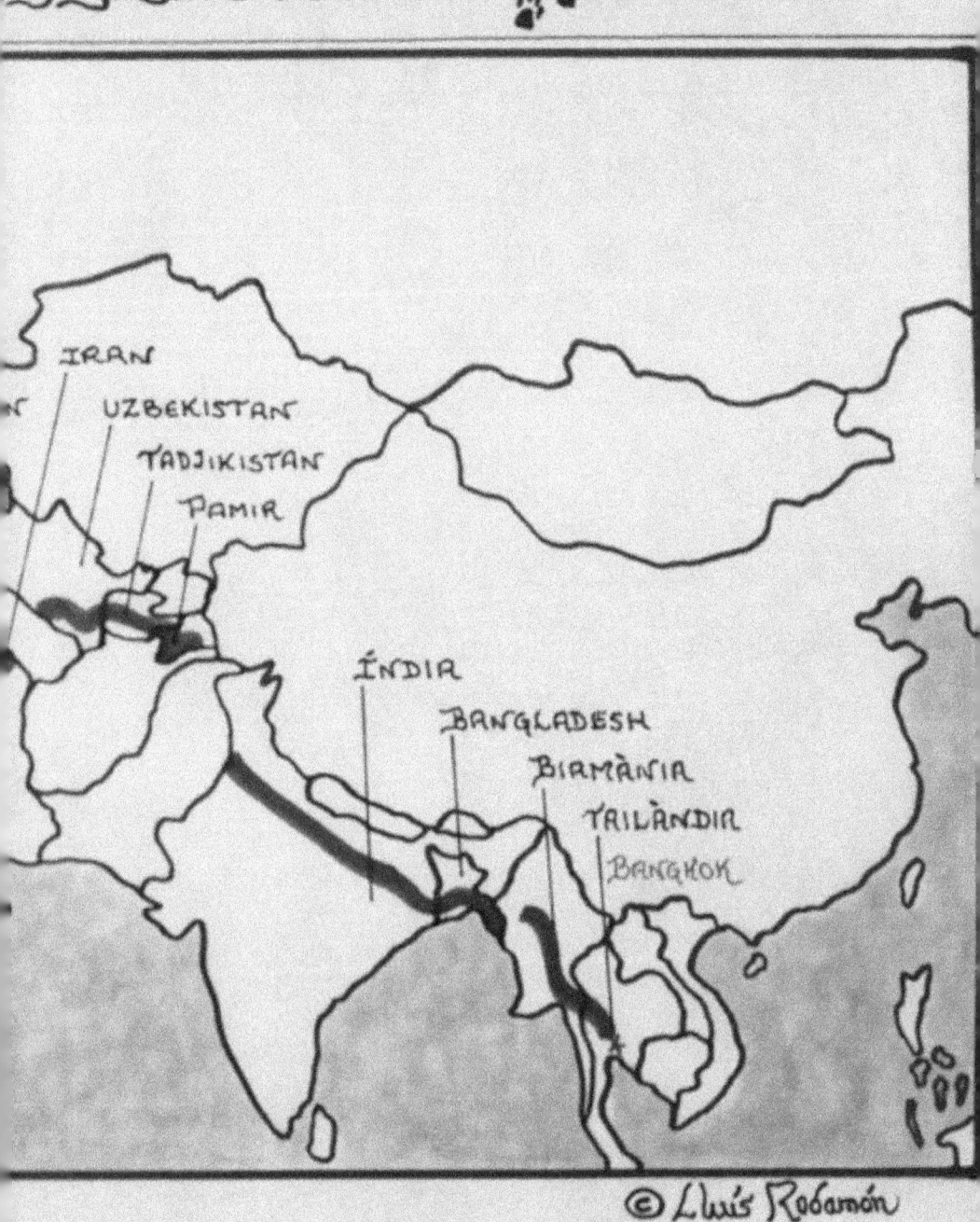

- IRAN
- UZBEKISTAN
- TADJIKISTAN
- PAMIR
- ÍNDIA
- BANGLADESH
- BIRMÀNIA
- TRILÀNDIA
- BANGKOK

© Lluís Rebamón

RESOURCES TO INSPIRE YOUR NEXT STEP

RESOURCES TO INSPIRE YOUR NEXT STEP

Bangkok Barcelona On Foot

Some of the stories or themes discussed in this book initially appeared as blog posts on our Bangkok Barcelona On Foot website.

You can read more about our adventure at bangkokbarcelonaonfoot.com.

A documentary about our walk and the kindness we found along the way was featured at eight international film festivals and, at the time of this writing, was presented at various conferences and events. You can watch the trailer at bangkokbarcelonaonfoot.com/documentary-documental.

Here are a few more quick facts…

We walked across Asia and Europe from January 2016 to June 2019. We were en route for 955 days and walked approximately 16,048 kilometers, or 9,972 miles. Extended, seasonal rest breaks are not counted in the total tally.

WE WALKED THROUGH:

- Thailand
- Myanmar/Burma
- Bangladesh
- India
- The Pamir Mountains
- Tajikistan
- Uzbekistan
- Iran
- Azerbaijan
- Georgia
- Turkey
- Greece
- Macedonia
- Albania
- Montenegro
- Bosnia and Herzegovina
- Croatia
- Slovenia
- Italy
- France
- Catalonia

RESOURCES TO INSPIRE YOUR NEXT STEP   149

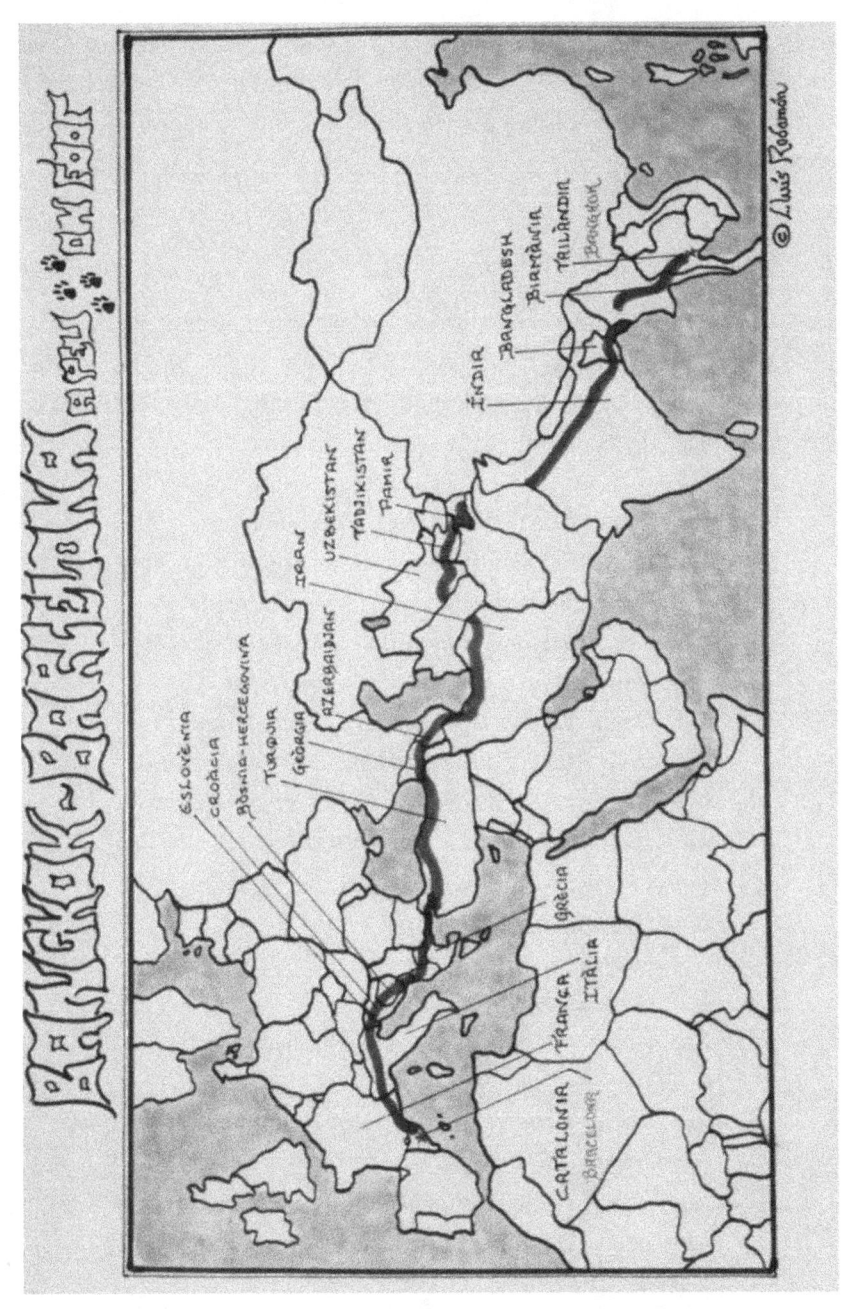

On a map, our route looks like this: *The Bangkok Barcelona On Foot route map, hand-drawn by Lluís, written in Catalan.*

Interested in bringing Lluís, me, and/or our documentary to your event? We would love to inspire your community! You'll find more information about us, the topics we speak on, and contact information at bangkokbarcelonaonfoot.com or jenniferbaljko.com/documentary.

EXPAND YOUR EMOTIONAL LITERACY

How fortunate we are to live in a time when emotional wellness is becoming mainstream and familiar. These are a few of the books that continue to inform, teach, and guide me through the emotional in between places. I hope you find wisdom in them as well.

> *Brown, Brené.* Atlas of the Heart. *Random House, 2021, and* The Gifts of Imperfection: Let Go of Who You Think You're Supposed to Be and Embrace Who You Are, *Hazelden; 1st edition 2010 (And almost anything else by her!). The quote in* The In Between's *chapter Courage: A Heart-Centered Choice to Act was found on her Facebook feed in this February 14, 2019 post, https://rb.gy/w78fq6*
> *Eckman, Paul and Eve Eckman, with the support of the Dalai Lama, "Atlas of Emotions" website,* atlasofemotions.org
> *Newby, Dan, and Curtis Watkins.* The Field Guide to Emotions. *2019.*
> *Newby, Dan, and Lucy Núñez.* The Unopened Gift. *2017.*
> *Ryan, Patrick Michael.* Dictionary of Emotions. *Pamaxama, 2014.*
> *Seltzer, Leon F.* "The Complex Emotion of Courage: Do You Really Understand It?", Psychology Today *website, 2015.*
> *Smith, Tiffany Watts.* The Book of Human Emotions. *First published by Profile Books Ltd, 2015;*

Published in association with Wellcome Collection, 2016.

Swoboda, Kate. The Courage Habit. *New Harbinger Publications Inc., 2018.*

ADDITIONAL NOTES

Definitions cited in *The In Between's* chapter Courage: A Heart-Centered Choice to Act were found in:

> Merriam-Webster Dictionary, *online at https://www.merriam-webster.com/dictionary/courage*
> Goodreads, https://www.goodreads.com/quotes/263728-courage-is-knowing-what-not-to-fear. *The quote is often attributed to Plato, but the exact origin is unknown. The quote reflects ideas presented in Plato's dialogues "Laches" and "The Republic."*

PINPOINT YOUR FEELINGS

I have found these emotional wheels to be valuable resources in understanding my own emotional landscape. May they serve you, too.

> *Calm, Blog, "The Feelings Wheel: Unlock the Power of Your Emotions"* calm.com/blog/the-feelings-wheel
> *VanMuijen, Abby,* avanmuijen.com/watercolor-emotion-wheel *and on Instagram* @avanmuijen. *A professional license to use and publish her emotional wheel illustration was purchased via* etsy.com/shop/AbbyVanMuijen.
> *Wilcox, Gloria,* allthefeelz.app/feeling-wheel

ACKNOWLEDGMENTS

I'm immensely grateful to everyone who has appeared on my life's path, helping me reach this wonder-filled moment.

To all my teachers, mentors, and guides, both living and gone, thank you for sharing your wisdom and being exemplary models worth following. My appreciation goes to my Townsend 11 writing friends, who first showed me how to turn wanderlust into heartfelt stories. My sincere thanks to Sierra Melcher and the Red Thread author community for being guiding lights as I steered this book toward a safe harbor.

Vivian and Paulie, you remind me daily of the importance of making good decisions. Jessica Goldmuntz Stokes, thank you for rekindling my forgotten love of labyrinths, and Mai Ling, for pioneering a path I didn't expect to follow more than once. Amy, your belief in our greatness extends far beyond that first job fair and continues to inspire me to aim higher. Sheelagh, our seasonal attunements keep my feet on the ground.

To my *Fierce Awakenings* co-authors and my Mindful Writing Mentees, you encourage me to be my bravest self. My SEEEO sisters, your tender embrace is invaluable when my courage falters.

Quim Badenes, thank you for bringing our Bangkok Barcelona On Foot tales of kindness to life as a documentary film, and Toni Arbonès, for sharing three years of walk-related stories on your uplifting "Els

Viatgers de la Gran Anaconda" radio show. To my backpacking friends around the world and everyone who invited us in for tea, you've taught me how to carry the weight of my heart on my shoulders.

Anna, thank you for showing me how to use my inner magic for the greater good. Jackie, Chris, Marissa, Dana, and my extended family, I cherish all the ways we journey through life together. Ascen and Lluís, your love gives me shelter. My mother, Janice, knew I needed something more from the world, and my father, Joe, showed me how to walk through the muck and pull myself to shore.

Lluís, holding your hand as we step forward is something I celebrate every day. *De mica en mica s'omple la pica.*

Finally, to those further down the road whom I haven't yet met, you are fireflies in my night sky. I'm walking towards you.

My cup is full, and you all keep filling it.

LEAVE A REVIEW

Reviews matter! They go a long way in helping prospective readers choose a book and determine if it is a good fit for them. Reviews are also the greatest kindness you can offer an author.

If you enjoyed this book and found value in it, please leave an honest and brief review on Amazon amzn.to/3XhD3fT and/or Goodreads.

ABOUT THE AUTHOR

JENNIFER "JENN" BALJKO

Jenn nurtures Joy Journeys and encourages fellow way-makers to embrace the fullness of their fierce, fun and fantastic lives. She does this as a mentor, editor, speaker, author, creativity kindler, and founder of Always On My Way.

Drawing on nearly 30 years of award-winning journalism, writing, and editing experience, Jenn guides aspiring authors through the early stages of drafting their book manuscripts. Most recently, Jenn guided a group of 11 women (and herself) through a nine-month writing and editing cycle; our collaborative book, *Fierce Awakenings: Calling in Courage and Confidence to Walk Life's Spiral Path*, was published by Red Thread Publishing and earned Amazon bestseller kudos.

As a certified mindfulness meditation teacher and licensed facilitator of The Emotional Institute's signature movement and embodiment experience, the Emotional Tour, Jenn holds space for the deep emotional release and healing that comes when we lower the volume of our racing thoughts and connect to our body's natural rhythms.

She counts completing a three-and-a-half-year, 16,000-kilometer walk across two continents, from Bangkok to Barcelona, as one of her most significant achievements. Completing this book is another one. :-)

Learn more about Jenn and her creative playground at alwaysonmyway.com and linktr.ee/jennbaljko.

- instagram.com/jennbaljko
- goodreads.com/jennifer_baljko
- amazon.com/stores/author/B0CJ4ZBRRJ

RED THREAD PUBLISHING

Red Thread Publishing is an all-female publishing company on a mission to support 10,000 women to become successful published authors and thought leaders. Through the transformative work of writing and telling our stories we are not only changed as individuals, but we are also changing the global narrative & thus the world.

www.redthreadbooks.com

See our catalog of books:
bit.ly/RedThreadLibrary

facebook.com/redthreadpublishing
instagram.com/redthreadbooks

READ JENN'S ESSAYS

"The Wind That Whispers to Me." *Fierce Awakenings: Calling in Courage and Confidence to Walk Life's Spiral Path.* Red Thread Publishing, 2023.

"Meeting Joy." *The Best Women's Travel Writing, Volume 12: True Stories from Around the World.* Travelers' Tales, 2021. Honorable mention, Fourteenth Annual Solas Award, 2020.

"Journeying: Bangkok to Barcelona on Foot." An online series of essays published on The Nature of Cities website, thenatureofcities.com/journeying-bangkok-to-barcelona-on-foot, 2016-2019.

"Castles in the Sky." *The Best Travel Writing 2008,* Travelers' Tales, 2008. Republished in *The Soul of a Great Traveler,* Travelers' Tales, 2017. Republished in *No Set Boundaries: Eleven Stories of Life, Travel, Misadventure, Volume 2,* by Townsend 11, edited by Larry Habegger, 2011. Grand Prize Bronze Winner, First Annual Solas Award, 2007.

"Finding My Rock." *No Fixed Destination: Eleven Stories of Life, Love, Travel Volume 1,* by Townsend 11, edited by Larry Habegger, 2011.

"Shampoo Sisters." *No Definite Plans: Eleven Stories of Laughter, Love, Travel, Volume 3,* by Townsend 11, edited by Larry Habegger, 2011.

"You're Going to Wear That?" *Chicken Soup for the Soul: Just for Preteens.* Chicken Soup for the Soul Publishing LLC, 2011.

ALSO BY JENNIFER BALJKO

FIERCE AWAKENINGS:

Calling in Courage and Confidence to Walk Life's Spiral Path

We all walk life's spiral path.

It is a journey pulling us inwards, upwards, and onwards, each time around to another expression of our highest potential. Fierce Awakenings give us the courage and confidence to be voluntarily vulnerable, bravely bold, and undeniably unique.

Twelve way-making women show us how they reclaimed their inner truth and stepped towards authenticity, belonging, and freedom.

- Discover what lies in the center of your lived experience
- Heal the wounds of your heroine's journey and rise above shame, pain and discontent
- Trust what calls to you now, and feel safe and empowered to take the next step.